Angelic Visitations

R.J. Manuel

Published by Ashley Brooke Publishing, 2020.

ANGELIC VISITATIONS

First edition. April 12, 2020.

Written by R.J. Manuel.

I dedicate this book to my gracious wife and my wonderful family for all their patience and support. And to the Lord Jesus Christ that saved my soul.

INTRODUCTION

This book is my testimony about me finding God and living a life with Angel's from Heaven and experiencing 40 years of Angelic visitations. It's about sitting down with our Heavenly Father and describing what I saw. Life-altering events to come that will affect the lives of all living things on the planet and future events that will challenge the faith of all people. For some, the realization of how little faith they have to face the Biblical events that are coming. And to those with no faith perhaps a time of reflection and soul searching. No one ever said it would be an easy walk for the obstacles that life would put in your way. My goal is that anyone that can read these words will minister to you, causing you to search and seek out the "Word of God" for yourself. Hopefully, helping you to find intimacy with your Heavenly Father.

With where I have been and what I have seen, it will be your flesh, and it's very reasoning that will battle with you to deny you of Christ. To deny God's very existence and the future to come and how what the Bible tells us could come from a loving and caring God. I pray that you can use this book to help you and your family to grow in your relationship and understanding of Jesus Christ. And that these words will take you on a new walk of intimacy with your God.

In writing about all I have seen in the prophetic from years of angelic visitations, this book represents only a small portion of that which is to come. I have had my share of struggles in my life with what you are about to read. My flesh was always reasoning, telling me all the wrong reasons why this was impossible what I was experiencing. How I lacked knowledge and wisdom for the spiritual battle, I was to endure. I want you to understand this; it would not be until later in my life that I would even begin to embrace and accept what I have seen. Often in my life over the years, my flesh would lead me to think this was a curse upon my soul. It would be this plague upon my life that I would battle for many years, trying to reason out what was happening. My reader friends, we live and exist in the flesh, and that of the spirit is far removed from everything distinguishable in the flesh. With Angels coming and going, Prophetic future events giving birth, where the world will change, and knowing people's lives will be changed forever, I was keeping my visions and angelic visitations to myself. I rarely shared them, and then with only a select few. Often finding my-

1

self challenged and feeling isolated to myself while sitting in church listening to sermons about end times. Knowing in my spirit what I had seen, I desired to live a healthy life, enjoying my family. I thought I was not God material nor capable of a godly life. Then God gave me this journey.

In the spiritual, some of you will question the truth because of what I reveal, you'll think that can't possibly be real. In the flesh, you reason visions and prophetic events can't really happen, so you say to yourself. You will wonder what "burden of the Lord" really means. I had never even heard the words "burden of the Lord" until I cried out for God's help and what it would mean to me. The spiritual meaning is compelling, and this you will learn. I consider myself just as ordinary as the next person. I wanted to enjoy life and family. But you will discover God can and will reach out and use anyone, He so chooses. In a conversation, I will tell folks, "God did not just have to bend my knees. He had to break my legs." As I was still crawling away from what God was calling me to do. I never had but one choice to make, that this journey was my life. And God had already predetermined for me the twist and turns I was to take. One thing I didn't know was the severity and the cruelty of the attacks I would come under in my walk to God. That the fight for our souls goes beyond man's human conception, and the battle rages day and night for the souls of our children and our families. In our world, man battles self to be his own God. Where peace today is easily found in our possessions, our accomplishments, money, and social status. Where our elevation of the material things become easily idolized in the world we live in. These things will make us easy prey for all that is not of Christ, and as such, the battle goes on. Where man finds contentment is only temporary. For man's desires of things for the flesh are controlled by a power far higher than his human reasoning. Without a relationship with God, you will find no peace. And you will never win the battle. The spiritual war that is going on around us, I never wanted to see it. It is dark, it's ugly and friends it's very real. From pages of notes, anything I could pick up to write on over the past 40 years, I would write and journalize about the angel's visits and what had happened. At times I would want to forget rather than remember the angelic visitations. It is overlooking those end of time events I had seen from these visits that I have seen the secrets of the Lord, and I have carried them. I pray that there will be an unveiling of the prophetic that you will see in these words that will lead you to get closer to your God. That there is a considerable strengthening of your faith taking place between those that read this and their God.

Angels, many over the years, many with different messages, appearances of power that could destroy an army but at the same time rock a baby in their arms. Yes, Angels with a size that could wrap around a car with unbelievable strength or stand with me with an incredible peace as I was shown events to come. Angels that could deliver a message in God's authority. Angels, messengers from Heaven above. Messengers sent from God. Angels, standing by your side in life challenging situations. Angels so divinely gifted, a member of God's elite, with a mannerism of a helping hand. Where the Kingdom of God is always lifted up, Angelic messengers know their place, and they know the Father. They are warriors that go beyond words to the unimaginable. Where there is no questioning this soldier's ability for whatever task the Lord has appointed. Only God could have created such a magnificent spiritual being for the many jobs before them. Angels brought here to help us as God's messengers and our guardians. They are real. This book is about you being alive on the inside with your Heavenly Father. This book is a survival manual to make you aware. It is preparing you and your family for the harshness of Judgment day. God's word has told us Judgment will happen. It will fall upon the earth and God's people. It is my prayer, that your faith and walk with God becomes stronger than it's ever been before. That the Lord will use these words to awaken your spirit. That these words you read are your notice to get closer to God through his only begotten son Jesus Christ. Keep your eyes on the Lord and never take them off of Him.

FOR GOD SO LOVED THE world that He gave His only begotten Son, that whoever believes in Him should not perish but have everlasting life.

John 3:16

IT WILL BE ESSENTIAL when reading this book that you read through your spiritual eyes as you begin to see into the prophetic world of events to come. I pray the Holy Spirit will reveal to you truths as you go deeper into this prophetic testimony, learning from God's nuggets in the words you are about to read...My testimony to you.

AND THEY OVERCAME HIM by the blood of the Lamb and by the word of their testimony, and they did not love their lives to the death.

Revelation 12:11

Chapter 1

God Had A Plan

So where did it all start? Well, if I look back, I could see things happening in my spiritual life, but at the time, I had no idea how much these events would affect my adult life. I can't call it naive, because when you're young, you don't know any better. Some events that take place will impact you for the rest of your life. Those events help shape you into the person you become. Again, these are events happening in our lives we wouldn't necessarily think about. At the time they were happening, maybe you were only ten or eleven years old. Do we even care about what this big world is all about when we are that young? For most kids growing up, it's about having fun and doing everything you want to do.

In my world, I grew up in what I thought was an average family. I was the eldest of four kids. When my mother and father got married, it was quite tough. My mother gave birth at a young age. My father was wanting to play college football, only to get hurt, putting an end to that dream. So when I came into their life, thank God there were no abortion clinics! If there was, I wouldn't be here telling my story. I would learn later from my mother that she had attended church and Sunday school regularly. I know God's word never comes back void, but I wouldn't learn how much that meant until later in life.

Looking back, God already had a plan for me. I never heard much about that moment in my early life. I would learn more about all that when my father was dying of cancer. There were terrible things said, could've been from the medicine, or the stress from dealing with death. I don't know, a lot of hurtful words were spoken though. As time went by with God's help, I learned to forgive him. I only share this in the hope that if one of you is struggling with a broken parental relationship, you will learn to forget about it. God does a great job

5

of healing our broken hearts if we let Him. What happened in the past, learn to let it die in the past.

I had a brother who was five years younger than me. He would die by the age of twenty. We got along great when he was younger, but as he got older, he was always into so much stuff. Life was a big party for him; he never stopped partying. Until he was killed later on. Those were tough times for everyone. I could write another book on his tormented soul and the 'party like there's no tomorrow' lifestyle he lived. Every day of the week was terrible; it was never-ending. The devil had him by the shirttail and wasn't letting go. Then I had two sisters, one much more responsible than the other, I suppose. They also were under terrible attacks in their lives. I have prayed for both of them, but for my own sanity, I had to lay them down at the foot of the cross. Oh, how it hurts when God steps in to make that knee bend. However, it's in Gods' hands. I've learned that God doesn't need me to micro-manage His affairs. Over the years, I've seen many people praying for loved ones to only end up full of torment in trying to do what only God can do. God doesn't need our help, does He?

For the most part, my family was a typical dysfunctional home with lots of alcohol and drug abuse. With two beautiful parents that loved and provided for their kids almost to the point where it would kill them.

This book is about 'Spiritual Warfare,' helping you to identify where evil finds the gateway into our souls. I pray as you read this, God leaves you nuggets that will help you along the path of life. God gives us free will, so what you do with those nuggets is up to you.

Thank God for good Grandparents. I spent most of my time with my grandparents; it was my getaway. I had a lot of fun when I was with them. Because it was tough in those early years, money was tight, so my father worked two jobs plus side jobs to make sure there was plenty of money coming in. Mom stayed home with the children; she was always loving and kind-hearted. My mother was the true definition of a 'Mom.' Since Dad was working all the time, and I was the eldest, I had more responsibilities around the house. Like carrying the coal from the coal bin to the old furnace, it was our only source of heat. Of course, most of my friends heated with coal. Some had oil heat, but in our neighborhood, most heated with coal. These responsibilities made me feel a lot older than I was. Mom would sit on the basement steps and supervise, making sure I had the damper right, and the furnace stoked up once it was going. Occa-

Life was getting better when my youngest sister was born. There were eight years between us. Because of Dad's hard work, he had become very successful in his business professions. We were in a couple of new houses, got new cars, it was all about letting the good times roll. It began to have a huge influence over what would happen within my family and the difference in how you looked at life. When compared to how my brother and two sisters were raised, there was just a big difference. My little sister was doing things at twelve years old that I wouldn't have even thought or considered doing. She grew up wide open with very little discipline. By then, money had become God. It was money, good times, work, family, and then God, that was the order of things. Well, not too much of God, and that was our life. What a difference a few years could make. When looking back, I can see where evil was already lurking, seeking to destroy lives. For the most part, we were your average hard-working family. We had our problems, but money and the good times made life enjoyable.

But I cherish those precious days of my youth even though at times they were tough. I remember a lot of powdered milk and regular milk thinned with water back in those early days. Back then, it worked, and you got by. I suppose it was why I always enjoyed going down to my Mom's uncle's farm. There was always fresh milk and great food at their farm. Plus my grandparents would go to the farm with us, just about every weekend. I had the greatest grandparents, mom's parents were my favorite, and they were always around helping us out. All through my life, they played such a big part in helping me to become the person that I am today. Sometimes, I wish I would've listened better to what they shared, and taken their advice more to heart. If only I would've. Nowhere does it say life is going to be easy, as the father and husband I am today, I ask, "Do we ever learn to rest in peace with the person we become?" God only knows.

FOR I KNOW THE THOUGHTS that I think toward you, says the Lord, thoughts of peace and not of evil, to give you a future and a hope.~ Jeremiah 29:11

DAD'S MOM HAD A FARM, too; my great-grandmother lived there also. My grandfather on my dad's side died young, and I never got to meet him. Though I did get to talk with his best friend several years ago. He had told me many things about my grandfather that I didn't know. I was glad to hear about him.

I often ask, where was God in all of this? Where was God in my family? Thank God for my grandparents, because they would play an essential role in my early learning of God's word, no, I'm not professing to be an angel or ever was one. I was just a boy growing up, loving everything good and fun. At this point, I might have said Jesus, who? Do we ever see the evil circling, waiting to destroy our families? Oh, how the innocence of our youthful life can be so simple, but as you will read, life can begin to change people and not always for good.

BE SOBER, BE VIGILANT; because your adversary the devil, as a roaring lion, walks about, seeking whom he may devour: ~ 1 Peter 5:8

Chapter 2

Grandmothers Prayers

When I look back, there are small pieces of my life that were shaped by the input of my grandparents and how I feel about God. Because of what I saw and what I shared with my grandparents, this is where my early foundation of God had its beginning. With my mom's parents, I would attend a Southern Baptist Church, and even though I was young, I still saw things that didn't sit well with me there. At an early age, I saw how my grandmother was treated at the church there were things she couldn't or shouldn't do. Today we know it as man's legalism, denominational rules, man's law to see God, control, the authority; you know what I mean. When they would be speaking from the word of God, I would say to my grandmother,

"Why does that man say you're not to cut your hair or you can't wear pants when we go out on the farm?" And I would ask, *"You mean we can't get to Heaven to see Jesus if you cut your hair?"*

I don't remember everything about those times, but my grandfather and I would enter the church with my grandmother made to walk behind us. We were in our clean white shirts with dark pants. I heard the man standing up there talking, saying this was how it had to be to see Jesus. Don't you think for a second, that this type of treatment of my grandmother didn't have a significant influence on how I felt about people at this church. Man and his silly ways of wanting to be on the same playing field with God. Even to this day, there is nothing worse than man and his hypocrisy controlling folks with so much legalism, in what they must do to see Jesus. I could name off so many silly ways and things I have seen over the years for you to get to Jesus created by man. Today looking back, I know God was showing me these things for a reason. I was only beginning to learn.

However, it was fun to go down on the river and watch everyone get baptized, and to this day, I consider that pretty special. Getting in that river when the water was cold, those folks would have a hard time standing up after they came up out of the water. The preacher would shout that the Holy Spirit will warm you right up. What was funny is I always heard so much talk about the Holy Spirit. Every time that preacher would talk about Him, I would look around the church trying to see him, and I never did see him. He would be down at the river, and people would start talking about the Holy Spirit, and again I would look everywhere to try to find him. More than once, that Holy Spirit had come into that church where he would knock a man and his wife right down on the floor. He must have been super fast because I never saw Him do it. Even at the river, it was as if He would jump out of the bushes, knock folks down, and they would go shouting, and He was gone, that fast. I would sit there at the picnic table and munch on some fried chicken as people were hollering at the Holy Spirit. Therefore, it never made much sense to me, when there was so much good food on those tables to enjoy. But the funny thing to me was, how that Holy Spirit sure did get around.

My grandmother after church, when my grandfather wasn't around, would say, *'Those men don't know what they're talking about.'* I could tell she might've been a little mad about something. But she was always at church, and she always prayed. It would be much later in my life when my grandmother was dying that I would find out that her family was of Hebrew descendants and when her family had migrated into Pennsylvania there wasn't a Jewish community at that time. The family had wanted to blend in with the other folks so they would become Baptist and other denominations. I don't know too much about them, but I'm learning more of my Hebraic roots and know that God's word tells us we are grafted-in.

YOU WILL SAY THEN, "Branches were broken off that I might be grafted in." ~ Romans: 11:19

WHEN I WASN'T GOING with my mom's parents, I was going out to my other grandma's and going to church with my uncle. We would walk across the back pasture, climb the fence, and be right there at the Presbyterian Church. I enjoyed Bible School there. And in their church service, the Holy Spirit didn't upset those folks. They were quite quiet. Come to think of it, sometimes I wasn't sure if they were still breathing, they were so still. They would talk about the Holy Spirit, but never did they shout at Him. Always figured He had gotten along better with these folks, more than He did over at that other church. But it was still fun to go. And when these folks ate outside, it almost was like you were at a restaurant the way they did things. That was ok; they had good chicken too. Back across the pasture, we would go after church. And if Great-Grandmother who lived with my grandmother hadn't milked the cows, I would get to help. That was fun! Feeding the hogs too, but with Sunday Church clothes still on, I had to make sure I changed so I wouldn't get in trouble with Mom. It was on one of those Sunday afternoons that Great-Grandmother began to talk to me about the Holy Spirit.

I said, "*I sure would like to meet this man!*" She looked at me, serious as she could be, and started telling me that this Holy Spirit had something He wanted to give me. That He had some special gifts for me.

I looked at her and said, "*You mean like at Christmas?*"

She just kind of laughed, and continued to milk that cow.

She said, "*Bend down here,*"

and with that, I bent down, and she squirted me in the face with that cow's milk. She started to tell me that the Holy Spirit was going to give me a big drink of something extraordinary.

When I said, "*I can't wait!*" she got this big smile on her face and said, "*Neither can I.*"

We put the milk on the back porch after it was poured into a big crock, that was where they made all the butter and cream, all the good stuff that came from the milk. And as if it was yesterday, I remember her calling for me to come into the room. There she was sitting in her chair, she told me to get on my knees and to lay my head on her lap. Great-Grandmother, she always wore an apron. Once I asked her if she slept in her apron? Can't say I ever remember seeing her with that apron off. She always had her Bible beside her chair, on her lap, or beside her bed. She would read from her Bible all the time. Lots of times, she would tell me the story about her father that had read the Bible every day. And when he came back from the Civil War, he had a reputation as a no-nonsense type of man of God that could handle a gun. I was never sure how God and handling a gun tied together, I just figured if they didn't believe in God, well, he would shoot them. Years later, I would learn that my great-grandfather had fought in the 49th Virginia Company E. That he and his brother had fought in the First Manassas Battle, one had been wounded and eventually died in Richmond of dysentery. My great-grandfather was shot during the Gettysburg and Antietam battles. He continued to fight up to the siege at Petersburg and was at the surrender at Appomattox. I figured if a man could carry his Bible through the Civil War and still be alive, that must be a compelling, powerful book. But then at ten years old, it did make me think about that book. Great-grandmother would talk about neighbors that had been slaves that stayed and continued to work on the farm for many years. Dad talked about a man named Max, born to a slave, and their family continued to live close. Max had taught him how to drive when he was a little boy. Something also I never forgot, out at my great-grandmother's garden at the end of each row, there would be piles of musket balls from the Civil War that covered the ground. She would just put them into piles. She would talk about the men all shot up and missing arms and legs and how bad it had been.

"If it weren't for God's word," she would say, *"I don't know how we would have gotten through it."*

Looking back today, I know those were priceless conversations about a terrible time of suffering and hardship in our history that we had shared.

GOD THE REFUGE OF HIS People and Conqueror of the Nations. ~ Psalms 46:1

WHEN GREAT-GRANDMOTHER called me to put my head on her lap, I knew it was a warm, loving, and caring Great-Grandmother that loved me and loved her Jesus. But still, I wasn't sure about the gifts and how I was going to meet the Holy Spirit. With my head on her lap, I couldn't see Him, but that was all right, those were very special times I got to enjoy with my great-grand-mother. One thing for sure is, that apron had all the good smells from butter and cream to homemade jams and jellies. Laying my head on her lap, she began to pray. Now I had been around my grandmother's enough that when they started to pray, you better shut up because the gates of Heaven were about to open up. Well, Great-Grandmother, she began telling me about the Holy Spirit and Jesus as she rubbed her hands on my back. The more she prayed, the better it sure did feel. Kind of like a popsicle in July or a glass of ice-cold water. And I mean ice-cold water too. The more she prayed and talked to Jesus and the Holy Spirit, the more I began to shake with chills like somebody had dumped a bucket of ice water on me. She prayed, and she talked about these gifts and how important they would be to help other people. She began talking about angels, the more she prayed. I think the first time she prayed with me, it seemed like just five minutes, but it had been more like an hour, or so she had said. I will never forget how I felt so comfortable, so happy that I would crawl up on the couch and fall asleep. That was to this day, a powerful prayer that touched the heavenly and called down the Holy Spirit.

It seemed if, after that, things changed. You know for a long time I wasn't sure what exactly was going on. But looking back, I knew my great-grandmother had been used by God in me receiving my gifts of the Holy Spirit. From that day on, any time I went to my great- grandmother's house, I wouldn't leave until she had laid hands on me. I would kneel as always and lay my head on her lap. Even if Mom and Dad were ready to go, she would look up at them and say, *"You all go on out to the car, I need to pray over this boy before he leaves."*

And oh, those sweet smells from that apron, that apron could be so dirty but never once did that apron stink. Every time I would get that Holy Ghost chill. Oh, how special that was. The Lord was using her in a mighty way. Sometimes other people would come to the house, and they might be feeling bad. Great-Grandmother would lay her hands on those folks and begin praying. They would open their eyes and have the biggest smiles on their faces. Some would say they had been to Heaven's doctor.

AND THE PRAYER OF FAITH will save the sick, and the Lord will raise him up. And if he has committed sins, he will be forgiven. ~ James 5:15

GREAT-GRANDMOTHER, she helped a lot of folks, something I remember, if the Evangelist man of God Billy Graham came on TV, there she would be sitting right in front of the TV. What a wonderful woman of God she was. Eventually, she fell and broke her hip, and she couldn't get out on the farm, so the farm was sold, and they moved into a new house that made it easier for her to get around in. But till she died, even in that wheelchair she would lay hands on me as I knelt before her, my head in her lap, and she would pray. Oh, how I miss her. To be so touched by such obedience to God with such faithful prayer. She truly had an intimacy with her Jesus. How special a person to have in my life as my prayer warrior.

My grandmother and great-grandmother had blessed me and taught me so much that I could write a book on all that we shared. It was the importance of this foundation and how it would save my soul. I knew these were God appointed, and God had given the word for me to receive from my grandmothers. Thank you, Lord, for these women of God and providing such Godly women into my life.

It would take their spoken words to pull me from the evil of this world that I would soon see. Perhaps you think I have overlooked the men of God in my family and their influence of sowing into my life. Unfortunately, there were none. How sad there were no Godly men to speak of. Oh, how much of this I see out in this world today. My grandfather on mom's side went to church, and that's where it stopped. Meant very little, if anything. My father went only occasionally, or when it was a special holiday or funeral. My grandfather on my dad's side was deceased, and the step-grandfather never went to church. But they would tell you they believed! The world had pretty well consumed the men in my life away from the church. Looking back, it would always take a family tragedy before they would become religious again. But it would never last. I call it religious because they never knew intimacy with God. They would all become consumed by the world until the day they died. Oh, how many families I've witnessed over the years tormented and divided by the ways of this world. How true the saying, "*No Jesus No Peace*" it should be "*Know Jesus Know Peace!*"

Regardless of all the prayers, I still would think, "*But God, I want to live my life my way, but that was not to be.*"

Chapter 3

Evil and Ugly Things Around Us

By this point in my young life, things were going alright. We were moving out of the city into the country. That new house was the biggest, nicest house I had ever been in. Dad was still working really hard. He had started up a small business on the side. So we didn't see too much of him. And if we did, he would mostly stay in his room, sleeping or smoking cigarettes. He had smoked since he was ten; he had told me. Eventually, that would kill him. The crazy thing he would always say, '*These things are going to end up killing me,*' and he was right. I was eleven, soon to be twelve. Most of the time, I would go with Dad when he was going to his evening job. He would be on the go, and we would make a lot of stops.

One night we had to go to Cornwell's Market to pick up a few things. Dad had pulled a paper bag out from under the seat of the car and took some cash out. While he was in the store, I grabbed the bag and opened it. It was full of cash in rolls with rubber bands and lots of loose bills. I was still looking at the money and didn't see dad coming back to the car. When he got into the car, he saw me with the money, and calmly said, "*What are you doing?*" As I was folding up the bag of money.

I looked up and said, "*Dad are we rich? I've never seen so much money; even my grandfather doesn't have that much.*"

He replied, "*Just some extra money I made for selling some stuff.*"

Quickly I remembered him saying, "*Don't tell your mother, I want to surprise her with something new.*"

With that said, I suppose I didn't think too much about it. It wasn't long after that when Mom and Dad had gone shopping and bought new furniture. We had never owned new furniture that nice. It wouldn't be until a couple of

18

months later when I needed a pair of socks that I went into Dad's sock drawer and saw another bag rolled up with a rubber band around it. Digging down
deeper into the sock drawer, I found many more bags rolled up with money in
them. We must be rich, I thought. I didn't say anything to Mom because I knew
Dad didn't want her to know. I was soon to be twelve, plus I knew I wanted that
new bike. Dad and I had gone out to Montgomery Wards and down to Western Auto, checking out the bikes. After we had left the store and gotten into the
car, I asked Dad, *"Are you going to pay for the bike with the paper bags of money?"*

He looked over at me like what are you talking about; I remember I almost
got myself in trouble. Quickly I said, *"You know, the bag of money you had under
the seat."* He then just kind of grinned and said, *"I'll take care of it."* so we went
on home.

It would be a couple of weeks before I got my new bike. I remember that
day well. Dad and I had finished up work and were headed home. Dad had said
he needed to make a stop and for me to sit in the car. We pulled up in front
of this building, and Dad got a box out of the trunk to carry inside. A couple of minutes later, Dad comes out and, with a big grin, tells me, *"Let's go get
that bike,"* and off we went. Driving away, Dad pulled out another one of those
brown paper bags and handed it over to me. *"Look in there,"* he tells me. This
bag had more money in it than the last bag. I want to insert here if you're wondering where God was in all of this. Well, who needs God when it's all about
the good times in your life? Evil was having its ways with the flesh of men.

All I can say is that it would be a couple of nights later when we had finished work that dad would make his usual stops. And on this particular night,
we had to go out near Route 50 to this motel. We had stopped there before, in
fact, lots of times, and he would grab a small box from the trunk. Sometimes a
small bag, but it wasn't like the candy bags, though. I called those candy bags,
because every time we got candy at Cornwell's Grocery or Boyer's store, they
would put the candy into one of those brown paper candy bags. One time in
the store, I had said, *"Look, Dad, they have brown candy paper bags like yours."*
Dad got pretty angry that night, I mean very angry. He told me I wasn't to bring
up those bags again, around anybody.

Probably wasn't too much of God anywhere in my life at this point. Very
seldom did I go with my grandparents to church anymore. Besides, I was twelve
and had other things to do. But I would still see them on Sundays for dinner

or to go down to my mom's uncle's farm to visit. I find myself thinking about this time period when I look back. Those were some great times for me growing up. I can't help to think about what kids are getting exposed to in this big ugly world today. Even looking back, I search for words on how my life would be changed. The devil plays for keeps to destroy and take away all that is good. Never underestimate to what length the devil will go to destroy a life or an entire family.

THE THIEF DOES NOT come except to steal, and to kill, and to destroy. I have come that they may have life, and that they may have it more abundantly. John 10:10

SPIRITUAL WARFARE IS as real as the air you breathe. Of course, at this stage in my life, what did I know about spiritual warfare? I would hear my great-grandmother mention it when she was praying over me. My great-grandmother knew something. I have to believe she saw in the prophetic of what was to come. I believe that God was using her to prepare me for my journey and the direction that life was going to take me in and the people that would be touched. Meanwhile, from time to time, I would check the sock drawer to get clean socks, of course. Every twelve year old knows how vital clean socks are. Glancing for a second longer, I would look at the brown paper bags. Dad was really busy, and while at work one night, he had told me we would be late getting home. That he had a bunch of stops, we would have to make. By now, sometimes, Dad would let me carry the box up to the houses we would go to. Some would be small boxes and others larger. Sometimes the people would give me those brown candy bags. I acted like I had no idea what was in it, but I knew it was filled with money. The fun part was dumping all the cash together, that was the best. We would drive all over town, sometimes even out to houses in the country or by the local country club. We would go to the nice part of town, then down into not such nice areas of town. It didn't matter; we traveled all over. There was an area downtown where most all the colored people lived; at least back then, that was what they were called. Dad knew a lot of folks in that part of town. In those days, Dad was one of the few people that gave the colored boys work. In fact, they could park Dad's work vans along the streets in that section of town, and they never got broken into. I guess you could say; I was learning a lot from my dad. Even in those neighborhoods, he also would collect those brown candy bags. They would see him coming and walk out to the curb to pick up the box.

It was on one of these nights we had to go back out by that motel again. This was ok with me because they had a restaurant in front named after a famous Confederate General, Lee Jackson, and sometimes we would go in and eat. They had amazing food, so I always enjoyed going there. But on this day, Dad pulled up at the side of the motel. As usual, he told me to sit in the car and wait. When we pulled up, standing outside in front of a room was a black-haired woman puffing on a cigarette. When dad was hopping out of the car, this woman says, "*I'm done for the day.*" Dad said something to her, and I could tell he was mad. She turned and went inside behind him. I thought to myself, what is this lady doing standing out in front of a motel room with her bra on that looked like it was three sizes too small. After like fifteen or twenty minutes had passed, I got out of the car and walked up to the motel door. I pushed on the door, and it was open. Peering inside, I could hear people talking, but it was very dark in there. The more I inched my way into the room, the room had this smell of stinky perfume. It was nasty. Looking into the room, there were sheets hanging from the ceiling across the room. I figured I could hide behind them, so I eased on into the room and moved down until I got down to where two sheets came together and I was able to see through the crack. I don't know what I was expecting to see but wow, did I get an eye full. Men were standing all around the room with big lights and movie cameras. And right there in front of me was that nasty woman that had been puffing that cigarette, having sex. They were filming her while she was doing it. Not quite sure what happened after that, whether I stepped through the curtain or somebody saw me, but the men looked at me. Then Dad walked out of the room with one of those boxes. The woman on the bed having sex said, "**Oh My God**!" when she looked up and saw me. Figured she must've known God too, cause she sure was talking to him while I was standing behind the curtain. That room got so quiet I think they all stopped breathing. Dad said, "*It's my boy,*" and told me to go out to the car! A couple of minutes later, he came out and just looked at me. "*What do you think* *you were doing?"* he asked. Taking a second to come up with the right answer, *"I thought you might need my help to carry out a box,"* I replied with a smile. The only thing Dad said was, *"I need to take this tape to get developed,"* and downtown we went. I had been to this place before and enjoyed looking around at the stuff they sold. Eventually, I figured what was out in front of this store certainly wasn't what was in the back of the store. Dad, he always went into the back with the man that worked there. A few minutes later, he would come out with the boxes, and off we would go to make our stops. Figuring Dad might still be a little mad for what I had done, I acted kind of dumb with him. I didn't want him to get too mad with me for what had happened. After we had left the shop that night and made our stops, the only thing Dad said about the entire evening, with one of those looks, that you understood or else part, *"This is nobody else's business but ours, do you understand?"* he said, and with a nod that closed out my evening, but I couldn't help thinking about what I had seen in that room.

Things quieted down over the next couple of weeks. I didn't go to the motel for a while, and the next time I went, it was at a different motel. But that was ok because they had a really good restaurant there as well. But most of the time it was at the other one. I went into the motel rooms, and it became just another ordinary day. Sometimes it would be the same woman, sometimes others. Dad said they were from the city, that they would shoot the 8mm film, and we would take it to be processed. Then it was made into movies. This was all before VHS tapes were made. Dad had extra 8mm projectors that he would rent to the people so they could watch their films and some he would sell to them. The business was booming. Dad drove a new Lincoln every year, and the new big house was looking real nice with all the bells and whistles. The legitimate side of his business was making big money. And the not so legitimate side, *the pornography side* of the business was booming too.

I remember when VHS machines first came out. Dad had ordered one, and we were the only ones in the neighborhood that had one. It was the size of a small TV back then; it was so big, it looked like a piece of furniture. Now it was no longer 8mm reels in the boxes but VHS tapes. In fact, there weren't video rental stores yet. But we delivered right to the doorsteps and the amount of money in my pocket, well, I didn't go without that's for sure.

FOR MANY WALK, OF WHOM I have told you often, and now tell you even weeping, that they are the enemies of the cross of Christ: whose end is destruction, whose God is their belly, and whose glory is in their shame—who set their mind on earthly things. ~ Philippians 3:18-19

IT HAD BEEN SEVERAL years by now, and things were changing. Dad had started to get away from the pornography business. Later, he would say it had served its purpose and that if he hadn't stepped into it with another successful businessman in the town where we lived, he would never

had done it. But isn't that hindsight saying, *'I wouldn't have done it'*? So life went on.

In the meantime, our family was coming under a lot of attacks from the devil. Things were starting to change. By this time, I had met my future wife, so life was good. But my family was under terrible attack. Can you really wonder why? The alcohol and drug abuse were awful. There was no God anywhere in the family. The dirty money, well it was about as evil laden as could be. I never told any of my friends about the pornography business. Never let on to anyone about anything I had seen or knew. While other boys were looking at girly magazines, well, I was looking and seeing way more than a magazine. How much more I can put here but won't. Evil was real. It was just that dirty little family secret that stayed hidden. Things were pretty much falling apart. Mom and Dad would travel and take trips. My brother would trash the house with his keg parties. Things moved at a pace that life couldn't handle. Soon it would come to that end. My girlfriend and I spent a lot of time together. The confusion and dysfunction were taking its toll. Thank God, that I never got into the drugs to the point of destruction. I was no angel, I saw, and I did. But thank God that foundation my grandmothers had built with Jesus had never departed from me. Folks never, ever, doubt the power of prayer. How much I realize that now when looking back. The more I stood on the outside, the more I saw the work of Satan destroying a family. It was out of control.

ENTER BY THE NARROW gate; for wide is the gate and broad is the way that leads to destruction, and there are many who go in by it. Because narrow is the gate and difficult is the way which leads to life, and there are few who find it. ~ Matthew 7:13

ON THIS DAY IN OCTOBER, two men would come to the door. They were detectives from the city. My brother had been missing for about five days, and we had heard nothing. Dad always said when he saw them approaching, he knew, he knew my brother was dead. He had been killed at a rock concert that weekend before. No one was ever sure of all the details. But the witnesses said he had been in a fight and was hit by an oncoming van crossing the parking lot. That he had cried out, '*I don't want to fight anymore, I love Jesus Christ.*' and then he was killed. He would die a martyr in his battle against the evil he had been under attack from all his life. See, it was bad. In his bedroom over his headboard, he hung a poster of Jesus on the cross, and at his footboard he had a poster of the devil hanging. He battled a lot of torment and medicated to the extreme to get away from it. But he would tell you. 'You can't believe in Jesus without believing in the devil.' How right this is. Before his death, there was a great man of God that was just getting started in his ministry that he had contacted to try and get help. Mom and Dad had tried and tried to help him, but unfortunately, they didn't know-how. My brother had read a book called **"The Cross and the Switchblade,"** written by Pastor David Wilkerson. In fact, I spoke to the pastor briefly. He had agreed to come down and meet my brother in Pennsylvania and take him on up to his ministry. My brother went but only lasted a couple of months. Even with so much torment in my brother's soul, till the day he died, he carried his Bible everywhere. The devil had his grip, and he wasn't letting go.

Mom and Dad would never be the same again. A spirit of oppression came over them both with severe depression, and things only continued to get worse. The name of the band at the concert he was killed at was "Black Sabbath." Don't think the devil doesn't have a game plan to destroy you and your family? Just put out the welcome mat and see what happens. Oh, how many families I've seen destroyed. But my brother's death would not be in vain.

By this time, I had gotten married, had a daughter. I gave my life to Christ, two years after the death of my brother. From his death, my family would come to know Christ. And we all lived happily ever after, not! Sometimes don't you just wish life was like a movie and all the happy endings?

I would have my own battles to fight, and the day was approaching that I would begin to thank my grandmothers once again for those prayers and that foundation they taught me. Mom, well, between raising my siblings, dealing with my father, and so many other things she had to deal with God did make her the strong woman she was. After my brother's death, she went to church to find her peace. My father eventually died from pancreatic cancer. In fact, we would lose five immediate family members all to cancer within two years. I was getting beat down by what the devil was doing to destroy our family. I knew Mom had to call out the name of Jesus for how much suffering and pain there was in the family. Looking back today, I know it was her faith, cause certainly only Jesus could have given her the strength to get through the attacks against the family. Oh, how weak our flesh can become. Lord, help us.

In prayers, I would cry out to Jesus, "Oh Great-Grandmother, how much do I need those gifts of the Holy Spirit that you told me about when I was so young." Oh, the power of prayer, God had a plan. It would be now that my life would take a peculiar twist. From this point forward, my life would never be the same again. I was about to meet an angel for the first time.

BUT THOSE WHO WAIT on the Lord Shall renew their strength; They shall mount up with wings like eagles,They shall run and not be weary,They shall walk and not faint. ~ Isaiah 40:31

Chapter 4

The Journey

I think I had put off writing about my journey with Christ because of pride, fear of condemnation, or shame, whatever the reasoning may have been. But then the Holy Spirit said the testimony I share would help others to overcome and find their walk in Christ, renewing their strength. Friends, I never considered myself anyone special. In my walk in Christ, I have learned Christ can use anyone he so chooses. It doesn't matter what degrees you have or how old you are. You don't have to be special in any way, God's in charge. You stand approved by your Heavenly Father and by accepting Jesus Christ into your life. Our walk in Christ makes us very special, a child of God from now until eternity. Why do we struggle to find the path God intended for us to go down? I believe it is because we are such stubborn people.

AND THEY OVERCAME HIM (Satan) by the blood of the Lamb and by the word of their testimony, and they did not love their lives to the death. ~Revelation 12:11

For God has not given us a spirit of fear, but of power and of love and of a sound mind. ~ 2 Timothy 4:7

WE HAD STARTED ATTENDING the Baptist church after my brother's death and praise God for the peace we found at that time. Please don't wait to call on your Heavenly Father only at times of need. Because He is there for so much more. Why does it take something so terrible to bend our knees? Believe me, it took a lot to bend mine. I didn't realize how hard-hearted I had become.

I pray you will learn from my experiences written within the pages of this book, how powerful the things of this world are to let go of.

It would be a little over two years since the death of my brother that our walk with God had started. My wife's obedience to the Lord continued, and she took the kids to church faithfully. Unfortunately, like all the other men in the family, I too eventually stopped. Besides, the warm and fuzzy was nice, but I had real-life issues to deal with. Oh, how blinded we can be. The start of a spiritual battle over my life was about to heat up. Without Christ, we are so weak. I didn't ask for it or want it, so I thought. See friends, I really thought I had a choice in the whole scheme of things. I laugh as I write these words. But at this time in my life, there was nothing funny about what I was experiencing. Over the years, there would be things that would happen to me. There would be times that I could sense things that I didn't see around me. There would be things I would hear when looking at people, but they weren't actually saying anything. My confusion over these things could be troublesome, to say the least. There could be folks standing close by, and I could feel their emotions. Funerals were like a roaring sea, awash in emotion. The bad thing was there was no one to talk to about what I was feeling or sensing. But I knew I was sensing something. I wasn't sure what was happening with me. But I knew something was going on.

When I was younger, I would go to a friend's house; he lived in a large old farmhouse. He would always talk about his house being haunted. The first time I went into his house, there at the bottom of the staircase stood a spirit. I asked my friend if he saw anything, and he said, "*No.*" I walked on past it, and it just stood there. After we had gone upstairs, I looked back, and it was gone. One day, while eating dinner with him and his family, his mom was talking about how she thought their home was haunted by some unwanted company. I told her what I had seen, and she asked the other kids if they had noticed anything. All of them said, "*No,*" and started teasing me for what I had told them that I had witnessed.

The next time I went over to my friend's house, his mother asked: "*Have you seen any more ghosts?*"

At first, I just looked at her. Then I replied, "*Yes, I saw it again.*"

She wanted to know if I would take her and show her where I saw it. Getting to the room beside the steps, I pointed and said, '*There it is, standing right there!*'

This would be my first encounter dealing with the supernatural. She told me this was an evil spirit, and I shouldn't talk to it.

I then pointed to the wall and said, "*It's coming through that crack.*"

"*What crack?*" she asked,

"*That crack in your wall*," I replied.

She said, "*I don't see anything!*"

The next time I went to their house, she had painted that wall and had hung a huge cross. For a while, I didn't see any more ghosts. But eventually, they did come back. I would point, and she would paint, and another cross would go up. After this, I never said another word to my friends about it. Eventually, they moved out of that house, and I went over and broke 18 windows to let all the ghosts out. The family that owned the house operated a successful shoe business in the downtown area, and the house was eventually torn down for a new subdivision to be built. The not so funny part was that my mom and dad had to pay for all the windows I had broken. In time I would learn that there had been a major Civil War battle fought there. I assumed those were restless spirits somehow locked in that house and property.

On Saturday mornings, my friends and I would ride our bikes to go buy candy, and we would go past an old abandoned house. Boys being boys, we would stop and walk-in. I remember only being in that house for a few minutes when a spirit appeared standing in the hall. I waved my arms up in the air, and the spirit disappeared. I'm not sure what happened. But I never went back inside that house again. This house was only about half a mile from my friend's old farmhouse that was torn down. So I figured these spirits had moved into this old abandoned house.

My wife and I lived in a lovely home where my first angelic visitation would occur. It was in the middle of the night that I was awakened, and there before me stood a huge angel. Do keep in mind since I had never seen an angel up to this point, any angel was going to be BIG. He radiated from head to toe, taking up half the wall where he stood. He was massive, with arms the size of a large tree trunk. He must've been ten-foot tall as he stood from the floor, extending past where the ceiling once was. I sat up in bed, and looked at my wife who was sound asleep. I figured this was a dream or something. I can't say I was scared or felt any fear, but I was mesmerized by what was in front of me. He began to speak, not as you and I speak, but I could hear every word he was saying. He began to tell me that he was the first of many others that would come. He said they would come to teach me, and I would understand in time what it was all about. And with that, he was gone. I woke up soaking wet from sweat, but the crazy thing was I thought I was already awake. I woke my wife and said, *"Did you see or hear anything?"* She shook her head no, and I proceeded to tell her what had happened. I didn't sleep for the rest of the night. That angel was the most incredible being I had ever seen, again considering I had never seen anything like this before. The strength that I perceived from that angel was like nothing of this earth. His head was just massive in size, proportioned to his body. It would take me several days after this visitation before I calmed down and began to think about anything else. Something I'd never forget. To put it into perspective for my readers, this would've been approximately forty years ago. What I didn't realize was my journey with God was just beginning.

FOR BY GRACE YOU HAVE been saved through faith, and that not of yourselves; it is the gift of God.~ Ephesians 2:8

I NEVER SPOKE OF THIS visitation to anyone besides my wife. I am no one in the eyes of God. I am a loving father of two and a husband to a beautiful, caring wife. I am not religious and pray I never become religious. I am a lump of clay being shaped into something beautiful and useful for the Kingdom of God.

It would be about two months or so before another angel would return. This time as I was peacefully awakened from my sleep. I sat up in the bed; this angel was slightly smaller than the first angel. He wasn't as impactful as the first angel. The first angel was more of a warrior, and this one had more of a peaceful feeling. The angel began to speak to me, telling me about things to come and what I would see. Up to this point, I never tried to speak to the angels, they spoke to me.

The angel said, "*There will be those that will come to harm and deceive you.*" With that, he was gone.

FOR HE SHALL GIVE HIS angels charge over you, To keep you in all your ways. ~ Psalms 91:11

THE ANGELS I HAD SEEN have been very masculine in nature. None have been threatening in any manner to me. But they had incredible stature, with great power and might in their presence. I am trying to describe the indescribable, something not of this world. Again, I woke my wife and told her what had happened. Friends, don't think I wasn't questioning what was happening to me, I often asked myself, "*What was going on?*" This is very important when looking back, and I want you to understand that if my walk had been where it should've been with God, perhaps my perception of the spiritual realm would've been better in understanding and absorbing what was happening to me. But it wasn't, and my flesh was all over the place. Honestly, I thought this was that middle-aged man crisis, and I was going through it way too early.

Thank God for my wife and her wisdom in spiritual matters. She was raised in Catholicism, then became Baptist. She read her Bible and studied God's word daily and was trying to help me understand what was going on. I also talked in general conversation about angelic visitations with another preacher, and there seemed to be a slight disagreement over the matter. I wasn't comfortable discussing the subject any further with him. These were challenging times for me. I wanted no part in any of this. But, trying to describe my angel encounters had never been easy. Men have struggled whether to believe or not believe in the spiritual world. So, how do you explain the supernatural, where man battles it's very existence?

Things were calm for about four months, which was great for me. Then one night, it moved in a completely unexpected direction. I was awakened to see what looked like a man sitting on the stairs outside of our bedroom, glaring at me. At that moment, I was immediately fearful of the safety of my daughter, who was asleep at the top of the stairs in her bedroom. I woke my wife as I was moving from the bed. She immediately saw the man moving from the steps into the living room going, towards our dining room. As he moved, I stood and followed him, and I immediately realized this was the spirit of a man. I saw him at a standstill, so I proceeded forward towards him as I got within about five feet from him, then he moved into the kitchen. I continued to follow him into the kitchen, and then he was gone. And no, I wasn't praying; I wasn't saying anything. I was without words that very moment. My wife was petrified over what had just happened. She ran up the stairs to check on our daughter while I checked every room in the house including the basement. My spirit was very angry, on fire to be exact. I couldn't understand how, or why I was feeling this way. I felt violated by this spirit coming into my space. I suppose I should've been scared, but I wasn't, it was more of what had just transpired. My flesh was trying to reason with my senses to comprehend. What I didn't understand was that my spirit man was in full battle mode. I was such a babe in Christ with a warrior mindset. My daughter, thank God, was still sound asleep in her room. My wife and I went back into our bedroom after I had reassured her we had no other unwanted company. Sitting on the bed,

I said to her, *"Remember what that last angel said?"*

She shook her head and said, *"Yes, He said they would come and test you or something like that."* I nodded my head in agreement.

THE ANGEL OF THE LORD encamps all around those who fear Him, and delivers them.~Psalms 34:17

WELL, I WAS SURE FEELING like things were a little out of control. We both laid back down in bed, but of course, with the light on. We talked about what happened, and my wife was looking up scriptures in the Bible to try to find answers. Immediately it reminded me of the other spirits I had seen in years past. The manifestation of the human form of a man is what was so strange this time. There were no eyes to be seen, and his legs moved as if walking, but he was gliding across the carpet. I kept thinking to myself, this is all from going to church and getting baptized? I don't need this in my life, I thought. Therefore,

I had no desire to return to church. I told my wife, "*No more Baptist Church for me!*" However, My wife assured me that God was in all control.

It was quiet for a couple of weeks, which was good since my wife was about to have another baby. That's what I wanted on my mind, not this spiritual stuff. We just don't get what we want, when we want it, do we? Everything is in God's timing; that's for sure. It would be on the next angelic visit when everything would begin to change. I was awakened with an angel at the foot of our bed. Like the other one, he also was quite calm. He wasn't as large as the first angel, he had a very soothing demeanor. I wasn't fearful since it felt like I was with my best friend. I moved to the end of our bed, not sure how I moved, but there I was sitting with the angel in front of me. What happened next is quite hard to describe, but for the very first time, I began to talk with this angel.

"*What is this all about?*" I asked.

He looked down at me and said, "*In time, you will understand.*"

"*Why me?*" I asked,

I will never forget the look on his face as He grinned and replied, "*Because you are* **chosen**."

"*And that spirit that came to my house, what was that?*" I asked.

"*You were told you would be tested; it was nothing.*" He replied.

I didn't say a word; I just sat on the bed.

Then I said to Him, "*We can talk?*"

He looked at me and said, "*We understand each other in a way that will make everything possible that is to come.*" Within that second, he reached out His hand, which was several times larger than mine.

"*We need to go,*" He said.

Not sure what actually happened, but at that moment, I was moving quickly through space, and the next thing I know, I'm standing on a cloud. He looked at me and pointed to the people standing on the sidewalk.

"Watch," He said.

It was in those moments I saw demons surrounding the people. He looked at me and pointed again; this time, all I saw was people.

"*Where are the demons?*" I asked.

"*You will learn, you will learn to see,*" He said, as He looked at me.

Within that very moment, I was back in our bed, sitting up against the headboard. Questioning, what was going on with me? I told my wife once again what had happened. Understand, too; I was getting to where I almost didn't want to say a word to my wife since I thought I was losing my mind.

THEN THE DEVIL LEFT Him, and behold, angels came and ministered to Him. ~ Matthew 4:11

ON ANOTHER OCCASION, my daughter, who was only three at the time, would begin to cry out at night, saying she saw a man all hairy around his face looking at her through the window. We told her that it was impossible because she was up on the second floor of the house. On other nights, she would scream out and say that there was a man standing in her bedroom holding a knife. She was terrified, and then we knew we had a problem. Also, one night while sitting down in the basement rec room with my daughter curled up on my lap and our cat next to us. I heard someone coming down the steps to the basement. Our cat intensely watched, turning his head to watch as if someone was walking by. After we knew the unsettling spirits were in our house, we began to pray to cleanse it of everything that wasn't of God. We had our Pastor come to pray over our home as well, that was very powerful. No evil could stay in our house after praying in Jesus's name, casting the evil spirits out. We never had another problem in that house after.

Our prayers had been answered, and life was back to normal. When seeing these evil spirits, it was as if something on the inside of me was ignited into a blaze of fiery rage, and I would automatically go into a battle mode. I had no clue what this uncontrollable fire was, that would just come up on my insides, what it meant? There was just burning in my spirit, wanting me to unleash a war against the demonic evil. Looking back, I didn't have the knowledge to understand how hard this enemy would attack. My flesh was working overtime to figure out what was happening in this spiritual realm. I had done some not so great drugs in my past, but I was young and quite dumb. I thought maybe this was some type of flashback? I don't know, but I definitely didn't like it. I even talked about going to have some neurological testing done on me. I was such a babe in Christ. My flesh wasn't comprehending things of the spirit. I was such a mess, trying to figure out what was happening with me. I was back in church; I'll say that again; I was *in* church! I wasn't on fire for the Lord, but I was going *only* just to please my amazing wife. Looking back now, I realize how much I needed a relationship with Jesus Christ.

This was the first of many times where my hands began to burn. My eyes were on fire, piercing into the darkness, where the evil lives. A Heavenly battle was beginning, and I had zero foresight as to how much my life would be affected. Soon I was going to meet God's messenger again. My life would begin to take a radical change.

THEN AN ANGEL APPEARED to Him from heaven, strengthening Him. ~ Luke 22:43

Chapter 5

Battle of Wills

Our family was growing; we were the proud parents of a little boy. My wife always said if we had a boy, she would name him after a man that had a heart for God. So Noah came into our family. By now, we had moved to a new home, and the family was growing, and for the most part, life was good. Life still had its ups and downs, but we worked through them. I hadn't had any angel visits for over a year, maybe a little longer. So I had made up my mind that this was all just an emotional experience. With the death of my brother almost seven years before and going to church, that my entire episode with angels had only been a traumatic experience brought on by emotionalism. I read that Religious endeavors could have a way of affecting people. Frankly, I was living for the world. I went to church on special occasions, and that was enough.

Several more years would pass before the angels would return. Sometimes I would mention them to my wife, and other times I wouldn't. By this time, I had gotten to where I had actually told the angels to leave me alone. They would look at me with the same look I'd seen before, and in their calm voices, they would say, '*In time you will understand,*' and off we would go. It would be around this time in my life that I began to keep a journal on the angelic visitations and what I was told. Eventually, it got so bad that I would write on anything I could find as if my life depended on it. It became a battle of wills on my part. Oh, it was so bad. Over the years, I had come to accumulate a box full of notes.

How grateful I am for my wife, as she truly is a warrior of God that saved my life during these spiritual battles. She had grown more in her relationship with Christ. She had the gift of an intercessor, and I was just rowing along. It would be about this point that we decided to make a move out of state. I suppose the Lord orchestrated all of this because things just fell into place. And we were on our way. Don't ever try and figure out what the Lord is doing in your life because your flesh will never understand. We have to go with it and trust in the word of God as our road map. We made a move, and all was good.

The children were being picked up and taken to youth groups and church events. My wife and I had eventually decided that we should try and go to church with our children. Even if I were working Sundays, we would attend during the week or Sunday nights. The church had a lot going on. And by now, I was more at peace with my angelic visitations. It would be during this time that God was not happy with my complacency with his angels, I suppose. Again God would intervene to get my attention. It would be called the "Dream Center". The church had purchased a large building to use for other parts of their ministry, and I was involved in helping to get the place ready to open. It so happens on this particular day I am about five levels up in the air on scaffolding hanging a stage light. When I look down from the light there on the scaffolding beside me is an older man with a big smile, and he says, *"How are you doing?"*

I look over at him and then down at the floor and ask, *"How did you get up here? I didn't hear you climb up, and I didn't even feel you on the scaffold."*

He replied, *"Well, I tried not to disturb you. I saw you were busy holding that light."*

I looked over at him and said, *"I'm getting down to get some lunch"*

We both climbed down, and I looked over at his tool belt and said, *"That looks like a brand new tool belt you have on there."*

He just grins and says, *"Yep, might say I just got it, thought it would be fun to wear."*

I just looked over at him and laughed.

"What are you going to work on?" I asked.

He smiles and says, *"Nothing, I came here to see you."* I look over at him.

"Yep," he says, *"I came to tell you, you can't run."*

My eyes grew wide as I glared at him, *"Do what?"* I replied.

"Once you've been called by God, you can't run," he said, and then he looks at me again and smiles. For a second I was speechless.

"How do you know?" I asked, with a little more perplexed look on my face. Honestly, I just wasn't sure how to respond to him.

"Well, I have to take off," he said without answering me, and with that, he stretches his arms out.

He smiles and looks over at me again and says, *"My wings have been bothering me,"* all the while stretching around as if he's trying to scratch his back. By now, the look on my face was one of total confusion. This man certainly didn't have any wings on his back. He begins to laugh, and walks toward the door, turns around, and again says,

"You can't run!" then out the door he goes.

DO NOT FORGET TO ENTERTAIN strangers, for by so *doing* some have unwittingly entertained angels.~Hebrews 13:2

I'M STANDING THERE completely dumbfounded over what had just happened. I thought this can't be real; somebody is trying to play a prank on me. Just as quickly as the door closed, it opened again and in walked the pastor.

I said to him, *"I thought you were the older man that just walked out."*

The pastor just looks at me and asks, *"Has anybody else been here with you?"*

"Only the older man that just walked out, it's a wonder you didn't bump into him," I said.

Pastor Dave just looks at me like, what are you talking about?

"What man? The only door is the front door, and I locked that, and anybody in here would have had to come up past me when I came in, I didn't see anybody in here," he said.

I sat down and just looked at him then began to explain what had just happened. The pastor told me it must be something pretty special for God to send a messenger like that. I know he said a lot more but, honestly, I was in such a haze after that, I couldn't think straight. God, why me? What is this all about? After finishing what I was working on, I left.

Once I got home, my wife asked: *"what's wrong with you?"* I replied, *"You won't believe what just happened over at the Dream Center."*

My wife, the Holy Spirit filled woman of God she is, looks at me with a big grin and says, *"Oh yes, I would,"* and she walks away grinning.

Things happen in a person's life that doesn't always make a good reason as to why. In my life, this would surely be one of those times.

Several months would pass, and things were quiet. I had talked with an elder at church, and he gave me a lot of insight into what was happening. It was at this time I had gotten to work and minister to some of the guys in the Teen Challenge Program. Addiction is such evil from the pits of hell.

It would be on a Friday night when my wife would tell me that she wanted to go to this revival meeting, at an auditorium, and they were having a guest speaker and thought it would be fun.

"Nope, I don't want to go," I said.

Anyways, as the old ball rolls, we ended up going. The place was packed when we pulled into the parking lot, and I still didn't want to go in. It was called the Rock Ministry. I told her that we were going to sit in the very back, and if things got crazy, I was leaving. We walk in to take a seat right next to the door, and the service begins. It didn't take long before the spirit was moving, and everyone was upfront. I see this girl upfront who was shaking so hard. I looked over at my wife and shook my head. The Lord knew I didn't mean it, but I made some remarks that were in horrible taste. Lord, forgive me! I continued to watch what was taking place as the Holy Spirit was moving. I soon was about to learn how God can have a funny sense of humor. Please don't think your Heavenly Father doesn't always have a purpose. That evangelist holds his hand up in the air, looks at the Praise and Worship team then tells them to stop. He looks at all the people standing and hushes them down. You can hear a pin drop in that place. He takes the microphone, shouts and starts pointing to the back of the room. Now, who do you think he is pointing right at?

I look at my wife, telling her, *"We're leaving."*

And again, the man upfront shouts out, *"You!"*

I went to move, and my legs were frozen; I couldn't move. It was as if this retractor beam had latched on to my body.

This man of God shouts *"The Lord has a message for you, He wants me to give you a drink."*

I shake my head and look at my wife, who is laughing. How do you laugh at a time like that? All of this and all I wanted was Taco Bell. Well, that man comes down off of that stage. I'm telling you I now know what it looked like when Moses parted the Red Sea. Folks moved to each side of the aisle, and I think some even stopped breathing. I didn't hear a sound other than my heart pounding in my chest. The man comes walking back and reaches for my hand, as if he was Jesus, my legs start moving. My wife and I walk to the front of the auditorium, she's laughing the whole time. The only thing I can think about is all those eyes looking at me. Once we got to the front, the pastor told me that the Holy Spirit told him to stop what he was doing, that he was to give me a drink of the Holy Spirit.

The pastor shouts *"When God moves on him to do something he has learned to do it. So I know God wants you to have this."*

I look over at my wife, she has a grin from ear to ear. I turn to look at this man, and he tells me this is for you from God. He puts his hand on my head, and I'm telling you there was this most incredible ball of energy that came down from my head and up from my toes that when they came together, I saw the glory of Heaven before my eyes. It was as if there was a prophetic explosion of energy charging through the universe, and it landed on me.

ABOVE IT STOOD SERAPHIM; each one had six wings: with two, he covered his face, with two he covered his feet, and with two he flew. And one cried to another and said: "Holy, holy, holy is the Lord of hosts; The whole earth is full of His glory!" ~ Isaiah 6:3

I NEVER SAW THIS ONE coming. I was out for about twenty minutes, my wife was out as well, and I was laying on the bench. Because of my size, a couple of guys had carried me over as I was waking up. I had never experienced anything like that before. Then I thought back to when my great- grandmother would pray for me and how I would feel. My wife and I were sitting there for about twenty more minutes when my legs started to move. Then I began to move a lot more to where I was shaking. I couldn't even sit because I was shaking so much. Unfortunately for me, it was the same thing that I had been sitting in the back of the auditorium making remarks about; the girl that was shaking. I think God had a point to make. Yes, I did feel bad for the comments I had made earlier. Well, I shook for about three hours. I was so Holy Ghost drunk in the spirit; it was as if I was floating on a cloud. It was an incredible place to be. One of the pastors came over and began explaining to me about the move of the Holy Spirit. He said the evangelist told him he had never had such a move of God, to command him to lay hands on somebody. Looking back, all I can say is, Thank you, Lord, for this man's obedience that day. My wife drove us home because my leg was shaking so bad I couldn't operate the gas pedal. That night I rested in my Heavenly Father's love. It was something I wanted to hold on to. God had a plan, and he was going to shake me anyway he had too.

It would be about a month later that I would have one of the most profound visits by an angel. This angel had a different appearance. That of a warrior, he was much more radiant in the energy that was flowing from him. Again I struggle to find the words to use in describing something that is truly indescribable in the physical. This was really a 'Where is the next fight,' type of angel. As he reached out to take my hand, within seconds, we had moved from several places around the world. When he spoke, there was never a question of what it meant or what was going to happen. He was precise and very exact as to what the outcome of mankind was going to be. There was a renewed understanding of what I was experiencing, and a greater revelation as to what would happen. The angel told me that my flesh would be exhausted when I returned.

I listened, then asked, "*But why show me these things? Why me?*" and he replied, "*In time you will know,*" and with that, he was gone.

After that night, I had begun to realize how exhausted my physical body was becoming after traveling in the spiritual realm, even after getting out of bed. In the presence of the spiritual realm, and when I moved through it, it battled my flesh. Sometimes it would be a couple of days before I was rested. Still, I would try to digest what I had been shown and journalize everything. I researched scriptures for wisdom and understanding. The battle never went away. I knew I had to go deeper with the Lord for Godly wisdom to even get through my days.

A couple of months would pass when a friend of ours had asked me to help him with some work. I could use the money since we were planning to make a move back to our hometown. It had been a couple of years since we had moved away, and several of our family members were battling cancer. Again, God knew where he wanted me. There was an Assembly of God congregation that needed help building a new church. What a wonderful place for the Lord to put me to learn. Well, it didn't take long for me to see the split in the congregation over the church building. In fact, it became a weekly ritual in how pitiful and petty the arguments that these folks would get in over everything. It was sad, I would think 'Lord, what is this about?' One day the pastor of that church and I were up in the top of the sanctuary, over sixty feet in the air hanging lights. It was a very peaceful morning, which had almost become a rarity when we were working. That morning the pastor had been able to share the battles going on internally within the church family. I knew this man of God had a load on his shoulders to carry. We had just finished talking, and through the doors came about eight women or so. Then the pastor looks at me, looks down at them, and says to me, "*Here comes a lot of trouble.*"

The pastor no sooner said that, and one of those women shouts, "*Pastor we want to talk to you. We're not happy about some of the colors for carpet and paint.*"

He just looked at me and shook his head. Now keep in mind he had to climb down off all that scaffolding to get down to the ground. I was sure there was a lesson to be learned here as well.

Shepherd's Flock

When I was above the sanctuary at the top of the cathedral, the Holy Spirit would just come over me. I wrote on the walls one day for this church to be blessed, as it had blessed my life at a time when I had really needed it. There was a lot of pressure to finish up the church. A couple of weeks later, the pastor had been working and had pulled his back. Unfortunately, there was so much internal fighting within the church that God wanted me to see how folks could get. The pastor had been working really hard. On that day, when his back had gone out. It was bad, and he could hardly move. I had helped him sit down in the auditorium, but the discomfort was too bad. He asked me to help him get up and walk outside to the picnic tables. Unfortunately, he wasn't having much luck, so I scooped him up into my arms and carried him out of the building and laid him down on the top of a picnic table. I know one of those angels was carrying us because it felt as if I was just floating. It wasn't too long before the ambulance was there to take him to the hospital. How sad I thought, Lord, why did this happen? It wouldn't be too long before I had my answer. I suppose again if God wants to use you to get a message across loud and clear, He will. I was sitting there with some folks from the Maps program, who traveled around in their campers working on churches. Then came that little group of ladies. Now some of these folks were the ones that would bring lunch over and that was nice, but today they wanted to talk to the pastor.

"Where's the pastor we want to talk to him?" shouts this woman.

I reckon this was her come to Jesus' day because the Holy Spirit moved on me to give her a reply. I do want to say the Holy Spirit was burning, and the fire in my belly was boiling. I looked at those folks and said, *"He's not here!"*

and almost before I finished, she goes, *"Where is he?"*

I looked at her and said, *"I never see you folks pray for your pastor, why is that?"* She just looked at me.

"Do you, do you pray for your pastor?" I asked as she was glaring right through me. But that armor was not going to be pierced.

"Maybe today is your day to start," I said.

"Who are you anyway?" she says.

"I'm the one that just carried your pastor out from the church to be taken away in a rescue squad because he had hurt his back," my eyes piercing through that woman's soul.

All in the same breath, I said, *"I think we should pray, and you're the one that God has told me to do it!"*

AND WE KNOW THAT ALL things work together for good to those who love God, to those who are the called according to His purpose. ~ Romans 8:28

DON'T YOU JUST LOVE when God drives that sword? It can cut to the marrow. The group stopped their daily complaining sessions after the pastor had gotten hurt, and construction work was able to continue. The church was completed, and God had me moving on. The pastor, a nice man, an incredibly hard worker, retired from the church almost immediately after it was finished. It wasn't what I had expected to see at a new church that was under construction, but I suppose that's why God had me there. I saw how easy it was for people to take their eyes off of God. They were looking to their fellow man to complain about doing God's work. When the reality was, the work on the church was between them and their God. God knows, doesn't He?

It would be after finishing my work on this church that God would send another angel to bring me a prophetic message, at the time I didn't understand. And it was a message that I would have a covenant with God over. The angel had appeared, and in a moment, I stood atop a mountain looking out across a valley. I was shown people wandering, people hurt, people moaning. And the angel spoke to me and said,

"*You will build an altar, and it will be built from stone, for you will be known as the Gatekeeper,*" the angel gave me very specific instructions on how this altar was to be constructed.

I quickly asked, "*What is it for?*"

He answered, "*You will know in time.*"

Over the years, seldom did a day go by that I didn't think about the altar the Lord had instructed me to build, with precise instructions on what and how I was supposed to construct it. I had to patiently wait for that day. I have learned what may seem like forever for us in real-time; in the spiritual realm, there is no time. In the spiritual realm, it's as if time is infinite. The spiritual realm is there, it exists, and it's not made for your flesh.

BUT, BELOVED, DO NOT forget this one thing, that with the Lord one day *is* as a thousand years and a thousand years as one day.~ 2Peter 3:8

I FEEL IT'S ESSENTIAL here to expand a bit on the visitations by the angels. Over time I would talk as if you and I were talking. I was always in the spiritual realm moving, traveling to where I was shown prophetic events. In some instances, it would be as if we were there as the events were taking place. It was all very real; what I would witness happening in the future. Early on, when the prophetic angelic visitations had started, I was told we could never be seen. We would cross from the spiritual into the present during our travels. At times the way my body would feel in the physical could become extremely stiff and a feeling of exhaustion. I want to point out, at no time in my travels was there ever any threat, concern for harm, or anything that was a tearing down of the Kingdom of God. They are God's creation, and they know this. They can do the task

before them. Different angels have different tasks that they are in charge of doing. When you think about your guardian angel, realize he can do what an army
of men can't. Remember, an angel is God's heavenly creation of taskmasters. It
can be a little overwhelming in the flesh, and that's an understatement. For cer-
tain, I have had my struggles. I have over 40 years of experience with angels and
never once had asked for any of it. Something else I need to mention, back in
the beginning when the visitations had started I would have an angel tell me
that if I didn't read much of what man had written about angels, that it would
be easier on me when learning. There was never any confusion, even in the beginning God had it all worked out. In the spiritual realm, I saw things of God
moving so differently than what we see and rationalize in the world around us.
I was working hard to die to myself, but I wasn't ready for that to happen.

It was after the return to our hometown one night that I would have another angelic visitation. It would be after I had sat with the angel, that a most un-
usual thing would happen. The irony of that is, it's God's messenger; he can do
whatever he needs to do to make things happen. After my visit, my revelation,
my chat, my heavenly talk, I honestly don't know how to label it, other than
it was a divine encounter with God. This was a Father-son, come to Jesus type
talk. It was the glory of Heaven; the ambiance of Heaven was radiating out. The
human flesh cannot stand before God like that. I will expand on this later. After that divine touch, I would take several days to recover. One night a few days
later, there came angels that began to play music. They were playing a flute, a
harp, and a mandolin, the most soothing, comforting Heavenly music. Since I
didn't know what music from Heaven really sounded like, this music was calm-
ing to my spirit and body. Again pretty miraculous tones that were touching
and healing my body and my spirit. The angel spoke and said, "*In time you will
understand the healing power of sounds from God's throne room.*" It would be on
the morning of the second day, after the angel's visit, that when I had woken up,
my body was no longer tired, aching, and pain-free. My eyes, that had literally
burned shut, had cleared up and the redness was gone. What a welcomed re-
lief to feel the way I was feeling. What a wonderful healing my Heavenly Father
had bestowed upon me.

I shared with my wife that I was feeling much better. And how the Lord
had used his music to heal me. She had been getting me wet towels to cool my
eyes. I was trying to write down and keep things in a journal, but often I would

grab any paper and just begin to describe what I had experienced the night before. What was so clear to me was that Jesus Christ really did save us from ourselves. God's word tells us everything we need about the coming future, and where faith is going to be tested. You must understand no one is guaranteed a tomorrow.

WHEREAS YOU DO NOT know what will happen tomorrow. For what is your life? It is even a vapor that appears for a little time and then vanishes away. ~ James 4:13

THEREFORE, YOU MUST find your peace and rest in knowing that Jesus Christ has provided everything you need to overcome. Anything that is evil in man was grown in the pits of hell. You are well equipped for the battle of your soul. Rejoice in knowing that our Heavenly Father loves us that much. It's powerful, and He is the maker and the creator. He has made all things of the Kingdom of God to work for us. He loves us so much. It really is comforting to know and to have the understanding to seek out God's intentions for our life. Moving through Heaven in unexplainable ways, I wasn't prepared for what I was about to experience.

AND I WILL GIVE YOU the keys of the kingdom of Heaven, and whatever you bind on earth will be bound in Heaven, and whatever you loose on earth will be loosed in Heaven." ~ Matthew 16:19

Chapter 6
Touch Them All Lord

This hasn't been an easy walk. This life of mine has been poked and prodded with everything the world could toss at me. I have lost houses, and even as I write, I am battling the demons of the flesh. I'm in no way one to cry in their self-pity. It has taken me years to understand and try to figure out this life of mine. I know the Lord will bring me through, but oh the struggles. Then I had to wake up and realize it's just life. The only peace in my life was Jesus, even with what I was experiencing in the spiritual, my flesh was still so weak. Today, many years have gone by, and I've learned it would be God and my faith that could help me find my peace. I've learned faith is not faith until it's the only thing you have to hang on to and ouch, what a painful trip it has been. It has been a trip full of many sorrows and questions like, why me Lord? With the riches of the world pulling and tugging you away from God, how easy it becomes to only see God on Sunday mornings. You say, "*Sorry God, I've been really busy.*" How easy it is to fall into all the things of the world. Oh, how guilty I was of that.

One night I had a beautiful lesson in humility. Painful at the time, but God used it as a special time of learning. We were in the middle of a Bible study at my house. We had fifteen people that came over along with another pastor and his wife. I had just finished shutting down my business, and honestly, I felt like life had become just one big cesspool of crap, and I was standing right in the middle of it. Have you ever been there? It's just not a happy place. There we are in the middle of the Bible study and who knocks on the door but the man to repossess my vehicle. I mean seriously of all times. I had been out of work for a while, and things were pretty tight. I had a packed house, and there, my vehicle is getting loaded up on a rollback truck. God's word is abruptly stopped. I was ready to crawl out of my flesh that night. After I had talked to the man, he was within his rights for what he was doing. I told the man to have a good evening and returned to the house for our bible study. You can imagine how much I didn't want to walk back in that house. Now, if you don't think walking back into the house was not a moment of humility, you are wrong. But stop here, that's my flesh talking. See, God knew what He was doing, and that evening was predestined to happen. When I entered the house, there was dead silence with all eyes looking my way. Some of the expressions on people's faces fell in between a loved one's funeral and a tax bill. But see, I had already had a lot of eyes on me from before so God had prepared me for this moment. I looked around and, with a smile, said, *"Praise God, I'm glad that's over with, now where were we?"* and everyone clapped praising God in agreement.

I looked at them and said, *"God is using that vehicle as a message to all of us here. I have been tormented trying to hold onto that vehicle, tormented by calls every day, tormented by sleepless nights, tormented by a spirit of failure, tormented by doubt of trying to hold onto the car, and*

tonight you saw that torment come to an end. I was trying to take charge and prevent the whole thing from ever happening. I wasn't trusting in God and his word about any of this."

NOW MAY THE GOD OF hope fill you with all joy and peace in believing, that you may abound in hope by the power of the Holy Spirit. ~ Romans 15:13

OH, HOW EASY IT IS to get weak in the flesh when we begin to feel the heat from the fiery furnace heating up. Yep, my flesh was shouting and carrying on like a mad man. But in my spirit, God was showing me how humility and his love brought my peace back. That night, we ended up having a fantastic Bible study. Everyone began to open up and share what they were going through. Many shared how much they had been keeping things pinned up on the inside. See it was 2009; the economy had slowed down, and a lot of people's lives were facing challenges. It turned out to be a great night of fellowship in the Lord. God showed up in an extraordinary way. Actually, you might say, God was already there on the porch in the porch swing, waiting for the party to begin.

That night I slept great! What a beautiful way for God to show up and reach down and touch so many people, while your vehicle was going out the driveway on a rollback. I began to feel so much better on the inside after this ordeal. Friends, sometimes we just have to let go and let God be God. If you're reading this and you're tired of sleepless nights, upset stomach, or just being troubled, then maybe you're reading these words for a reason. Stop it, let go of it, and let God take control! Just believe and set yourself free of those problems. Sometimes letting go and allowing God to work can bring such a sense of peace back to your life and family.

There would be another opportunity that God would once again get to deliver a powerful message. Let me say this friend, when your Heavenly Father comes to drive a message home it's almost as if you can feel those iron spikes that were driven into Jesus' body in yours. It's not pretty, and it's going to hurt. On this particular occasion, during this awful economic downturn, I had to take my business into bankruptcy. There was an electric bill that had been transferred over to my home from my office. I had no money, and therefore the house electric got shut off. It would become the wood stove and my wife's smell good candles that would give us heat and light. Now let me tell you those candles weren't meant for the pioneer life-sustaining function. When we began this endeavor of living in the house without electricity, I had this idea of finding the old hurricane lanterns we had. You know the ones you set around for looks, in the hope that you never have to use them. After gathering several, I began looking for something to fill them with. Well, the only thing I could find was potpourri oil, and this is not what you really want to use to fill up your hurricane lamps. To make matters worse, I eventually broke every hurricane globe we had. In conclusion, we really weren't set up to live in a house with no power. It was in the very middle of winter and 18 degrees outside. The only thing I keep saying was how could a power company get away with doing this to folks. When I didn't go down to pay the bill, two days later, the power company sent a man to check if I had rigged the meter. Can you believe that? However, being without power would last a couple of weeks, and I didn't expect that I would be battling a utility company. But see, I was not there alone; this is where God comes into the picture. Lord, why is this happening to me? No, not me, Lord. At this point, I was just about out of firewood for the woodstove, but I learned that dry Barnwood burns just as good. You're telling yourself this just can't be happening, but it was. We had some friends bring a generator to use, and another couple helped me to cut a load of firewood. One day while out walking down the driveway, our neighbor stopped to say hi and asked: "*How are things going?*" Pride can be an ugly beast, so I never let on what we were going through. See, my prideful flesh didn't want to let go. I just smiled and said, " *fine.*" She was upset and started crying, and she told me that her mom was unable to get oil delivered for her furnace because of a hundred dollar past due bill. I mean really, are you kidding me? God, what is this? Her 85-year-old mother was having to choose between her medicine and heating oil. All of a sudden, our situation didn't even matter. Immediately my wife told her where she could go to get fuel assistance. And meanwhile, I gathered a couple of five-gallon cans, to put some kerosene in, and this got her through the night until the oil delivery truck could come the next day. In this same time frame, God would show us another situation. A mother and her two children were huddling around a kerosene heater because their power had been cut off in the middle of winter as well. What was God showing us? Was it how cruel this world was becoming? How could these utility companies get away with this? Doesn't the Bible teach in God's word to honor the widows and children?

We eventually got the power back on. But in those couple of weeks, let me say that everyone from the Governor's office to the House of Representatives to the Senator's office and finally the Utility Commission all were called. Friends, it was time to find our "**Boldness in Christ**" and begin to take a stand and take back what the devil has stolen. It would be from this experience that God would use this to show me things to come in the prophetic. This would show me just how harsh this world was about to get.

There's something else I have to share also. Over the years, as I was dealing with things and experiencing what I saw in the prophetic, it was the word of God on TV that helped me. It was as if that word of God would be divinely given at just the right time coming from the TV. Words that God would be sending to me, words that would pick me up. Yes, this was about the word of God given out and getting received by someone that so badly needed it. God has given us the power of discernment, and when I received it, I drank. It would taste awfully good. I probably can't remember all the different ones that I watched and listened to. But I can tell you there was a night while listening to Pastor Jessie Duplantis that God gave me a word right when I needed it. Or the time when I didn't care to put one foot in front of the other, and Pastor Kenneth Copeland and his ministry had picked me up and gave me a fresh breath to live. Or how Brother Hagen would minister to me those days after an Angelic visitation, to help me understand. Or on a day when Pastor TD Jakes got on there, and I heard God speaking the very words, I needed to hear. And how many times would I see Pastor Marcus Lamb and his wife Joni on TV, lifting up people and sharing encouraging Words from God. God used his man, Paul Crouch of TBN, many times. When my wife was in tears, how Joyce Meyer was used by God to lift her spirit up. Jentzen Franklin and so many more, I could go on and on. It was about the Word of God getting received at a time it was needed. I'm not about who teaches this or that doctrine or belief. I am about the Word of God that is given out when it is needed. And I thank God for the countless number of pastors that have come and gone in our lives. Men of God, sent by God for a message or a season. All these folks have been used in a powerful way to deliver God's Word at such a perfect time. They have saved the souls of hundreds of millions of people. Vessels used of God, for Kingdom work, thank you, Lord, for their obedience. The world hates the light of Christ and those that do work for God's Kingdom. The "Spirit of Division" is wanting to have its way.

It would be while in the middle of dealing with more of life's challenges that again God would decide to intervene. One day in the middle of helping my son with a project, there was a disagreement, and God would take His prophetic revelation and begin to bring it to reality. A revelation was given to me some twenty years before.

A MAN'S HEART PLANS his way, But the Lord directs his steps. ~ Proverbs 16:9

YOU SEE, I HAD MY THOUGHTS on how to do a job, my son had his, and since they weren't in agreement, it was time for me to depart. And there was a little bit of anger in the air, it happens. Before I left, my son's crew were putting some stone on the back of my truck. Frankly, they couldn't get it loaded fast enough, as I was ready to leave! It was not turning out to be a good day. What I didn't know was that God was already sitting in the truck waiting for me. I just love it when He does it when you're least expecting it. The most incredible feeling came over me. The Lord began telling me this was anointed stone specially ordered from the highest of Holy places. That this stone had been made especially to build His altar, which I had been given a prophetic revelation about 20 years before, with specific instructions of how the altar would be built. Now, with a truckload of stone, I'm driving down the Interstate playing some Shekina Glory Praise Music, and wham, the Holy Spirit smacks me so hard I had to pull over. It was as if the Glory of God filled the cab of the truck with like a bluish and gold ambiance aura of lights. For a while, I don't even think I was aware of the cars and tractor-trailers passing by me. I do love when the Lord takes charge like that. Eventually down the road, I came through the gate of our driveway and out to the field I went. Out there stood the cross I had been instructed to build when we first bought the place. Now, this is how God works. Something that was evil and causing division in my day was turned around for the Kingdom of God to bring about a predetermined destiny from years before. Gathering the stone off of the truck, I started to work on that altar that the Lord had told me about. It was as if God was standing right there beside me. The miraculous here is that the Holy Spirit was directing me. He knew how the rocks were to be placed, which rock was to be His anchor or corner rock. He knew the length, the width, and how the altar box was to be built. And He knew the precise placing of the stones for the burning of the altar fire. The weight and size of those large rocks were nothing as if I was lifting feathers. I had no idea what this was all about, but I was in God's hands and trusting Him! So I'm busy working when I hear this horn start blowing, it's my wife. She comes pulling into the driveway and gets out of the car, and I think the Holy Ghost hit her. She was shouting while holding onto the car door and praising God. Immediately she comes out to the field to see what was going on. I had told her earlier about the disagreement and that I was coming home to bring a pile of rock and that God had said, "*This was no ordinary pile of rock.*" And so there I was, what a day it was turning out to be. Well, God, what's next? Sometimes the hardest part about working with God is God has His own time and way of doing things. Have you ever gotten like that in your life, waiting on God to give you an answer?

SPEAK, LORD, FOR YOUR servant hears. ~ 1 Samuel 3:9

WEEKS LATER, ONE OF the angels I hadn't seen in years came to get me. This angel is the one that was the biggest, boldest, strongest looking of them all. I had pretty much gotten used to seeing myself asleep in the bed as I was moving in the spiritual when the angels would come. The angel takes me to the top of the mountain west of where I live. Let me insert here this is the same mountain where I had been with this same angel years before in a visitation and shown this abandon country church and told where this church was, is where I was to live, and sure enough, that church lined up directly with the house we eventually bought when we moved back to our hometown. He told me that I was to erect a cross in the field behind my house, and eventually build the altar. Now, back to the top of the mountain with this angel. Directly below us where we were standing, looking out across the valley. I was looking down, and I saw thousands of people sitting, others wandering around this abandoned country church. In the distance, I could see a flame shooting up in the field. The angel looks at me, telling me that it is the altar flame, and this is what I am to do. That I am to wear sackcloth and gather the ash from the altar fire. That I am to lay a shofar beside the altar. That there is a walking stick called a 'Moses stick' that I am to have out there. That I would fast for three days and nights. That the altar fire would burn cedarwood and that the fire must not go out. And I would be given the day when this was to happen. The next morning I wake up, and I tell my wife I need sackcloth. Not sure of what sackcloth meant, I call a friend of mine, a wonderful couple that has a ministry of helping missionaries overseas. Paul confirms what I was thinking, some type of rough burlap material. He tells me what the Bible has to say about it. In short here is what Wikipedia describes as Sackcloth-

' Sackcloth came to mean a garment, too, made from such cloth, which was worn as a token of mourning by the Israelites. It was also a sign of submission (1 Kings 20:31-32), or of grief and self-humiliation (2 Kings 19:1), and was occasionally worn by the Prophets. It is often associated with ashes.'

With that, I am off to the Southern States store to find burlap (Sackcloth). You have to keep in mind when God tells you to do something, you do it. On that day, it was burning so deep within me to find that sackcloth. And after several stops, I still didn't have any. I go to another feed store, and he tells me no one uses burlap sacks anymore; everyone uses plastic sacks. Then he remembers he does have a pile of old burlap sacks piled up outside in the mud from when they had cleaned out the buildings.

He looks at me and goes, *"They're really muddy, and they stink too!"* He must've thought I was nuts from the way I was grinning. I walked out to this pile of mud and manure and I can see some pieces of burlap sticking out. The whole time I am thinking, God couldn't we have done this another way? Keep in mind at this point, I have been crying in the spirit to retrieve this sackcloth regardless of what it took. I started to dig the sackcloth out from the pile. The man walks out on the porch at the store, laughing and shaking his head.

He shouts out, *"You must need that burlap pretty bad,"*

I looked over at him and shouted, *"If only you knew!"*

The smell in the car driving home was so bad! When I got home, my wife walks out on the porch as I'm pulling the muddy pile of smelly burlap out.

"What is that?" she asks. I tell her this is the sackcloth that God has given me to wear.

She says, *"Maybe you better talk with Him again to make sure, cause that's some stinking nasty stuff,"*

and I replied, *"This is it; this is what He gave me!"*

So I went and got my big trash can, got the garden hose and laundry detergent, and I proceeded to wash out the stinking burlap. Again asking, *"God couldn't we have done this another way?"* After an afternoon of washing, I had enough pieces of material for my sackcloth.

AND SO IT SHALL BE: Instead of a sweet smell there will be a stench; Instead of a sash, a rope; Instead of well-set hair, baldness; Instead of a rich robe, a girding of sackcloth; And branding instead of beauty. ~ Isaiah 3:24

TO HELP BRING THIS puzzle more together, it had been about seven years before this day of getting the sackcloth. It was late one day as I was leaving a construction job site standing below a 200-foot tall tree with roots sticking out of the ground. All of a sudden, the Holy Spirit told me to cut off a piece of this big root sticking above ground. Again when the Lord tells you to do something, you do it. I wasn't always like that. Remember, God had to break my legs to get me to this point. So there I am, it's getting dark, and I am cutting and chopping a piece of this root that is growing out of the ground at the base of this 200-foot tall tree. Hence, my 'Moses Stick' is birthed. Then the Lord gave me this revelation to understand about this root I was cutting. That we are grafted into the base of something so much larger than the flesh can ever understand. As big and mighty as that tall tree was, it was supported by many roots deep in the ground. So my 'Moses Stick' was part of those roots that support that tall and mighty tree, the same as it is within the Kingdom of God.

So my stick was gathered seven years before it was to be used at the altar. I reckon you can say, We really are a peculiar people. At this point, I have always been very guarded about sharing what has been happening between God and me.

Now about the Shofar. It would be on another one of those angelic visitations that I was told to go get a shofar. A shofar was to go out by the altar. Not having a clue where to find one, I called around to a lot of places. I would eventually find one at a bookstore fifty miles away. It was one that had been waiting in the store for a year. The owner of the store told me she knew it would be for the right person. Well, friends, God knew that shofar was for me. Because of that meeting and getting my shofar, we would meet a great bunch of friends from the Tribe of Judah Church Ministry in Boonsboro, Maryland. A Messianic Spirit-filled group of people that have become like family to my wife and I. The pastor is gifted with the blowing of the shofar and has an awesome Shofar Ministry nationwide. God had orchestrated this part of His plan for what would take place at the altar. God was definitely at work. My shofar calls out and touches Heaven with its sound. It is the sound of the presence of God, and the sound we use to cry out to God when we need God's intervention. He knew the shofar would be needed. All of these pieces were coming together that God has ordained for the altar. It would also be during this time that God had another surprise. God would bring a man and his wife, both pastors, into my life at the exact time needed. What a meeting God was bringing together. They had come up to the area looking to buy a TV Station. In the meantime, God had other plans. God would use this man and his wife for this season to come to the altar and share God's words.

Chapter 7

God Almighty

When the angels appeared to take me on a journey into the spiritual realm, we would be moving, traveling; was it through dimensions or through time, I don't know. Let me explain when I say we were moving. It's not like you and I move, it's like you're sitting still, and things are moving past you. It's like the world is standing still as we move through it. There is no time in this space. Here time doesn't exist. When I make references to crossing over, there were, in some cases, where there might be several crossing overs to get to where the revelations I've seen take place. I know you're probably saying, how is this possible? My friends don't try to put God into a box; it still won't help the flesh to understand in the spiritual. Please understand I am trying my best to describe what goes beyond what the flesh can comprehend.

In most cases, a period of many years would have elapsed in the world while in the spiritual realm, it had been back to back revelations. Without looking at this through your spiritual eyes, the supernatural I have been experiencing to this very day is challenging, even on my physical person, it has been hard. Understand you will be in a battle between the reasoning of the flesh and your spirit person.

That which is born of the flesh is flesh, and that which is born of the Spirit is spirit.~ John 3:6

There will be times that your fleshly reasoning will want to set in and make you question those things that you've been shown or have heard from the Holy Spirit. There will be people who won't want to believe, so choose carefully who you share your experiences with. Be prepared for those that will want to discredit your experience as pure emotionalism. Beware of the 'religious' ones, too. Guard yourself. God will let you know when and who you are to share with. I'm talking from years of experience here. You may be bursting at the seams to tell the world, but it will become obedience on your part to God to listen to what He is telling you to do.

BUT THE NATURAL MAN does not receive the things of the Spirit of God, for they are foolishness to him; nor can he know them, because they are spiritually discerned.~ 1 Corinthians 2:14

THE NIGHT I WAS TAKEN to be with the Father had started off the same as many of the other nights that I've traveled with the angel. Except for this time, I was taken vertically rather than in the same horizontal flight that we mostly took when crossing through time periods. This night I felt like I was traveling an incredible distance, or so I thought. We moved upward and then came to sit on a ledge of a large plateau. The angel looked and smiled.

I said, *"Have we traveled a long distance?"*

He replied, *"No, it was more to prepare you."*

"Prepare me?" I said,

"Yes, Your Father said to bring you. It is your time to speak with your Father," He said softly.

For what seemed like a long time, but I knew it wasn't. I said nothing and just looked at the angel.

The angel then said, *"You have helped us to feel your compassion and emotion over these many years in your time."*

HE continued, *"Time moves differently for us, and as you have learned to move through the realms, you too, have learned."*

At that moment, the angel turned then began to back away slowly, bending forward as if out of respect, and in the same second of space, there was incredible energy of light.

AND HE CARRIED ME AWAY in the Spirit to a great and high mountain, and showed me the great city, the holy Jerusalem, descending out of heaven from God, having the glory of God. Her light was like a most precious stone, like a jasper stone, clear as crystal. ~ Revelation 21:10-11

QUICKLY I LOOKED DOWN as if shielding my eyes from the Glory of Heaven before me. Just as softly as the angel had spoken, my Heavenly Father spoke. The glory of God's energy radiating around me. And at that moment, He spoke as a Father would to his son. Describing this is very hard. For such a special moment as this, How does a person even prepare? You don't. This is our Heavenly Father, who loves us.

Now listen up here. All the religious stuff of man is gone. Am I really going before my Heavenly Father, how special? If you don't believe that God is real, you are blinded by your own flesh and distortions of this world. I sat and listened intently. His voice, as I heard, was very gentle, authoritative, loving as a grandfather's voice might sound. A voice of concern and compassion for the little one before Him. God laughed. In that space of time, he began to explain to me why I was there, what was happening, and the things that were to come. In a flash, we were standing out in the universe looking at the stars and the planets. Mostly we were looking at Earth. At the same moment, God spoke about man and what mankind was doing in his fall. He encircled the planet as if it were inside a capsule. There was a picture once that I'd seen of this exact illustration, so I use this as the best description I can give you for what I saw. Then it was gone. As miraculous as this meeting was, for me to speak the exact words as spoken by God, I will not do that. I paraphrase and use only my words in describing our meeting. I do pray that the Lord is giving me the words that need to be seen in this writing as I recall this special moment.

HE said, "*I created, and I can take back. I am God. Man's mind was not made to understand the spiritual world. His emotions have led him to greater self-destruction. Man's treatment of his brother has only gotten more evil as man has continued to evolve.*"

HIS tone and HIS words are those of a Father concerned about HIS children. Again, I was returned back to where I was sitting on that ledge, and I could see across the universe of the Heavens. I'll use a description of pages in a book, to explain what I'd seen. Each page with its own beautiful universe stacked on top of the other. Surely the Heavens have many levels. The Father spoke, "*What man,*" HE paused and with that, I heard genuine and threatening anger. Like our earthly Father, I heard a parent upset and mad.

The spirit of the Lord continued to speak, "*What man has destroyed on earth, the animals that man has slaughtered. Man, his wars all in my name they butchered young and old, without conscious or remorse for what they have inflicted upon their brothers,*" again there was a pause. "*I have reached out and loved and given much where man didn't deserve another chance, I have healed, fed, and provided all that man would ever need, and man has sought to destroy all that was good,*" and then it was quiet.

And God spoke, "*They come to control my people. They come to lay waste to all that I made good. Was man's freewill the gate to his own destruction? Did I watch man grow to evolve into much more than he could handle? I have allowed how far man would fall away. All man had to do was believe and trust in his Heavenly Father. Was it not that which was sent to help him control his darkness from himself? I love my children. I am their Father.*"

Then HE paused as if a large breath of Heaven was taken in. "*You have seen the destruction of man, you have seen all that is evil that will come against man. And you have been shown the good that can come to mankind, the reward and the discoveries to cure and make mankind well. Tell them these things you have seen. Let man decide. Will it be his own destruction, or will man choose to live with that which was created for him?*"

There was a long pause at this point. In the spiritual realm, I was beginning to feel as if I was draining of life.

The Father spoke, "*I am their God, and for this, they will be given new light to bring the light of their Heavenly Father into all places. And for a time to come to their depravity and darkness shall be stopped. And in these times, they will be given the love of their Father, and be brought back into the largest gathering man has ever seen. And it shall be in this time my children shall find their torment will cease. They will have great healing and abundance of all that is good for mankind. Man shall be given discoveries, that shall bless man beyond his dreams. Man shall show repentance and be given his last chance to gather and rejoice before his Heavenly Father. And this will be the last time before the return of my son Jesus Christ their Savior. What mankind does with this period of Grace is up to him, so be it. After that time, the torment of judgment shall fall. And those without repentance*" *shall be judged into the pit of hell. So it shall be. For I am God, and you are a gate-keeper that I have chosen to deliver this message,"* and then it was silent.

WHEN I SAY TO THE WICKED, 'You shall surely die,' and you give him no warning, nor speak to warn the wicked from his wicked way, to save his life, that same wicked man shall die in his iniquity; but his blood I will require at your hand.~ Ezekiel 3:18

THE ANGEL RETURNED, and at that moment, I was back in bed wide awake. How fast things had moved after that are hard to describe. I fell out of the bed and was staggering around on my knees. I could hardly stand to get back into bed. My entire body was aching and hurting so bad. The thoughts in my head were overwhelming, trying to comprehend what had just happened. My eyes burnt as if they were on fire. I could barely open them. My wife woke up and saw me on my knees beside the bed, struggling to get words out of my mouth. She thought I was having a heart attack. With her help, I managed to crawl back into bed. I was again struggling to bring my eyes into focus to see her face as my hands were reaching out, caressing her face trying to reason what had happened. She put a wet cloth on my face to cool it and tried to bring some comfort to my eyes. It seemed as if I'd just gone to bed, but the clock said it was 4 A.M. I laid there in bed, trying to tell my wife what had taken place, but I was having a hard time talking. So I grabbed some paper and a pen and began to write down a description of what I'd experienced the night before so that it would be journalized. I slept very little the remainder of the night, perhaps in shock of the prophetic encounter I'd witnessed and the simple fact my entire body was aching so bad. I want to tell you that the next day was a glorious day, a spectacular day in the Lord. Perhaps full of praise and glory for what I had witnessed. But unfortunately, it was not. Still short on words to even describe to my wife my prophetic experience. In fact, I hurt so bad I couldn't even go to work. I was mostly lying around and taking aspirin. It would be later that night that the Lord's angels returned to minister to me with healing music again. These angels were different, and the heavenly music was so soothing to my spirit and flesh. Soaking in their presence was divinely peaceful.

The angel spoke and once again said, "*In time, you will understand the healing power of sounds from the throne room.*"

Upon waking, from such a deep, restful sleep, the next morning, my eyes were no longer sore. The aches and pains in my body were gone. I felt like a new person. What a wonderful healing my Heavenly Father had bestowed upon me, absolutely incredible. Now friends, let me ask you this. How do you go about trying to have a normal life when you know you've met God the Creator of the universe, and all of mankind? Don't make a self-diagnosis because it won't be good. What did I see? I saw a Heavenly Father that loves his children so much. A loving Father willing to give his children compassion for what they don't deserve. A Father that warns us about disobedience, to save our souls from the coming destruction. Oh, how much he loves us!

It's been a while since I've read this journal writing since this experience happened to me. For a time, I was reading over it about every day and sometimes more than that. I know my Heavenly Father gave me the correct words I needed to share with others. I've learned over the years how God works and that there is absolutely nothing impossible with God. Even after these many years, my body is a little worn from all that I've experienced.

All I know for sure is that the Lord had given me this assignment, and I was to carry it out. However, I didn't know that this task was to span 20 years before it would come to be fulfilled. Again we want to reason about time in our flesh.

So now I was entering into a prophetic time when all the required items the Lord instructed, had been gathered and ready to be used. The Lord had given me a specific time as to when I was to begin His work. I received confirmation from some sweet friends of ours in Christ. The Holy Spirit had given them word and instructions about the starting time frame which confirmed what I'd been shown. He is also the man God used to provide me with great insight into the sackcloth and ash, as prophetically given to him through the Holy Spirit. God was at work, and He had a mighty plan that had been in the works for approximately twenty years. I can tell you that for a couple days before the lighting of the altar fire; my spirit was just alive with the glory of God. I'd begun praying and fasting with juice and crackers a few days before.

The Holy Spirit was filling me up for the day that I was to light the altar fire. I was busy cutting up cedar wood, to get ready to start the altar fire. I started on a Thursday evening and ended on Saturday night. Over those three days and nights, my God and I began to share an incredible time of prophetic insight. The Lord took me under his wing to show me great mighty things about the world.

CALL TO ME, AND I WILL answer you, and show you great and mighty things, which you do not know. ~Jeremiah 3:33

THESE WERE SPECIAL times. I'd learn about our world as I walked with God's messengers He had sent. There was one moment where I was praying out at the fire and had dozed off. I felt a warm breath on the back of my neck. I woke up to find it was my black Lab Jack sharing my space, thank you Lord it was not a bear. While kneeling before the altar fire going deep in prayer, I was overcome by the Holy Spirit, and Heavens Fire started washing over my flesh. Oh, during those moments when I was there to spend time with my Heavenly Father, my flesh would struggle with reasoning, unable to understand the Holy of Holies. Although I was doing what God had called me to do. Then I heard the Holy Spirit say, "*The fire burning at the altar will be used to minister and touch people in different ways.*" When God has spoken to you, and you realize the vision that you were given is coming to fulfillment, the devil will use your act of obedience will to still cause the flesh to try and reason out, question, and deceive you from completing the task before you. That's when you need to pray for God's angels to surround you and protect you. Knowing that you are under God's covenant and doing His will. When you have that divine calling, rest assured that you 've already been equipped with the tools that you will need, so stop worrying. Perhaps you've been blessed in secular music, and God is calling out for you to use your talent to begin to minister to others through a spiritual music ministry. Is God calling you, telling you it's time to use your spiritual gifts to help others? God has seen your tears. You can't keep taking and not want to give back into the Kingdom of God. It is your obedience that moves you closer to God. Just have faith, trust God with the vision or calling he has given you. If your act of obedience to God were to be interpreted and understood by everyone, then God would have given everyone the same vision. God has a divine plan and has chosen you for this appointed season. Feel free to contact me to share what you are being called to do. Fear not for God is with you.

Have I not commanded you? Be strong and courageous. Do not be afraid; do not be discouraged, for the Lord your God will be with you wherever you go." ~ Joshua 1:9

The Holy Spirit began to take me deeper and deeper into a very intimate place with my Heavenly Father.

HOWEVER, WHEN HE, THE Spirit of truth, has come, He will guide you into all truth; for He will not speak on His own authority, but whatever He hears He will speak; and He will tell you things to come. ~John 16:13

POVERTY

The Angel of the Lord took me on another journey, and it was as if the Lord was beginning to weep, it was like a splash of an ocean wave. When it hit the ground, my legs would tremble at each drop. Almost immediately, I was standing before a gated enclosure, and I could see thousands of people just walking around. What was this place, I thought? It was as if the people had been drained of all their emotions. Their faces were expressionless. And I began to understand. This is the world's answer to living in poverty. This was a place where people from all countries around the world were being brought to. Placed in a camp with a controlled environment. How awful, I thought, moving them to enclosed camps, where they could be fed and controlled. Then I heard a loud blast and those stricken in poverty poured from a large number of buildings row after row of buildings housing the poor of the world. They were trained like animals coming to a whistle. How big was this place, I wondered?

And the angel of the Lord spoke, *"Look closer for their time has come and gone, they shall never know their Father."* I was confused by what the angel had said. And in the next second, I was standing in line watching the people. Their minds now controlled only by those that were controlling their food. And then the angel pointed out, and at that moment, I understood what the angel had meant when

He had said: *"they will never know me."*

It was then that I saw this large group of people and realized how all these poor souls had been forced to take the mark of the Antichrist. What would you be yielding to if you were hungry and your children crying with hunger? As more of the world becomes impoverished, how easy the control of the people will be. The angel began to lift us up into the air. The higher I got above the rooftops, the more buildings I could see. People were as far as I could see in every direction.

I asked, *"What will man and his society evolve into?"* *"What will become of man before the Lord's return if all things that were once Holy are gone?"*

The angel began to speak, *" A man was made without limits. Man can increase and learn in knowledge and wisdom beyond what man can even think now. A man was created with infinite wisdom to always learn. A man was made perfect. Man's desires can be limitless without boundaries. And when I created the woman, I made that which would be perfect for one and another in an ideal world. But we see how sin has made his heart dark and evil. We understand how man has lost his control over contentment for those things that were good. How many generations have been lost? Only one more time will man have the chance to know Me."*

Then it became quiet, ending the revelation. The sweet smell of the altar fire fills the air around me. I know it is the Holy Spirit taking me deeper. I add more wood to the fire and kneel to pray again. Then as if a mighty angel had scooped me up, I am standing there beside the angel.

THE REVELATION OF JESUS Christ, which God gave Him to show His servants—things which must shortly take place. And He sent and signified it by His angel to His servant John, who bore witness to the word of God, and to the testimony of Jesus Christ, to all things that he saw. Blessed is he who reads and those who hear the words of this prophecy, and keep those things which are written in it; for the time is near. ~ Revelation 11:1-4

DEMONIC SPIRITS WEAKENING The Church

As I stood with the angel before two large podiums inside a huge sanctuary. It had no ceiling; the stars of the sky were the ceiling. There at each podium stood a pastor.

The angel began to speak, *"They both love the Lord, they both know the Word. They have both done many wonderful things for the Kingdom of God. They have treated their people well. They were blessed in the work they had done."*

With that, the angel raised his hand, and we began to move forward in time. I could see the pastors as their faces were aging, and their hair had turned gray.

And the angel began to speak, *"Watch as brother turns against brother. You will see them fight over their church members. All in the name of God, they will declare. Their love of things in this life is their most prized possession. Soon they will become as gems trampled into the dirt by a spirit of Antichrist. Their faith stripped away. They will find no peace in their hearts. And so they too will die a tormented death for turning their backs on the Kingdom of God."*

NOW, THESE ARE THE ones sown among thorns; they are the ones who hear the word, and the cares of this world, the deceitfulness of riches, and the desires for other things entering in choke the word, and it becomes unfruitful. ~ Mark 4:18-19

AGAIN, THE ANGEL POINTED towards the podium. People were standing, praising God, their spirits lifted up into Heaven. There was a peace I felt as I stood there and listened. And there before them the purest of pure, Jesus, he was sitting, listening and watching. What a beautiful sight to behold. I wanted to move; then, the angel pointed towards the other podium. The noise, the racket, terrifying noises, sounds not of God. I stood and watched what was happening. There was a spirit of anger over the entire lot. A spirit called "Division" was causing the people to separate, and they were each singing a different song.

"What is this?" I cried out.

"Once these were good people, I know they loved God. But because they love themselves more than God, they have fallen away. Self never stopped challenging the word for authority. Nor did they ever die to self and acknowledge the Kingdom of God. They became tormented by all that was evil that has come to take them away," the angel said.

BUT KNOW THIS, THAT in the last days perilous times will come: For men will be lovers of themselves, lovers of money, boasters, proud, blasphemers, disobedient to parents, unthankful, unholy, unloving, unforgiving, slanderers, without self-control, brutal, despisers of good, traitors, headstrong, haughty, lovers of pleasure rather than lovers of God, having a form of godliness but denying its power. And from such people turn away! For of this sort are those who creep into households and make captives of gullible women loaded down with sins, led away by various lusts, always learning and never able to come to the knowledge of the truth.~ 2 Timothy 3:1-7

THE CONTROLLING SPIRIT of the Antichrist had already fallen upon them. I could see something different about them. They were moving in strange ways as if their body was contorting. They were shaking violently as if a fever of emotion had taken over their senses. The sounds they were making were awful, almost a demonic sound.

The angel spoke, *"They feed on their own emotions, you have seen these spirits before, they are not of the Father, again, feel their spirit."*

I began to feel a spirit of everything around me being worshipped as a God. The people there were worshiping everything around them. I could feel the emotion, the spirit as if coming from everything I was seeing. What was this, I was feeling? At that moment, the angel of the Lord raised His hand. The emotion and the spirit I was feeling was gone.

Again He began to speak, *"That is the spirit in man to worship the things of man. Confusing spirits will come to destroy all people. This will bring only evil and harm to those that once loved the Father. They will turn on each other like a pack of dogs outside the city gates. Their flesh will starve them of all Holy things. An empty soul only to perish in a slow death, tormented by the controlling spirits. Into the fire of hell will be their home. This will come to pass, for the Lord is coming. I am coming to my children. So it shall be."* I woke up and prayed for the rest of the night.

BEWARE OF DOGS, BEWARE of evil workers, beware of the mutilation!~
Philippians 3:2

WATCHING THE SUN COME up, I knew what the Lord had shown me; that the Church can not sleep. That our adversaries are working around the clock to destroy everything we know as Holy. Without respect for the Church or the pulpit, the House of God will become nothing more than a social club where anything goes. Oh Lord, what will it take for us to remove the blinders and wake up before it's too late. To deepen our faith in our walks with Christ Jesus. Oh Lord, we do so love you. Oh Lord, does it really have to happen like that? Will our brothers and sisters in Christ turn on each other with such tormented spirits. Their ways become so evil, so blind, never to see you. Again I heard the Lord say, *"For you have found that which has always been and forever will be, For I am God."* I continued to gather more wood, maintaining the altar fire.

The glory of Heaven was powerful that second day. Rain clouds were coming. But that didn't matter; it was the obedience to what God had instructed me to do. I knew God would give me the wisdom to keep the fire burning under the downpour. It was in all this pouring down rain God began to touch me again. I had the fire protected. As I began to go deeper in prayer again, an angel appeared. There was an incredibly loud noise overhead, and we were standing looking out across a wide strip of land. You could hear the sounds of a lot of jet planes cutting through the air. And the angel of the Lord raised His hand, and all was silent.

Then I heard the voice of the Lord say, *"This is the land that was given to Israel, this is where I will return, this is where mankind shall know I am the beginning and the end."*

And with that, my legs were shaking beneath me as the ground was shaking.

And He spoke again, *"The first war will not last, the adversaries of Israel will realize the Glory of God dwells here, and too much will be lost. It will never be the same after this. Boundaries will be changed. Those that will come again from the land of Egypt will try. But again, they will know Israel is Holy. The might of the world will be against all that is good in Israel. It will not last."*

AND IT WILL COME TO pass at the same time, when God comes against the land of Israel," says the Lord God, "that My fury will show in My face. For in My jealousy and in the fire of My wrath I have spoken: 'Surely in that day there shall be a great earthquake in the land of Israel,~ Ezekiel 38:18-19

THEN WE WERE LOOKING out across a broad plain standing on the edge of where a valley was. And there I was shown a beautiful stone, the surrounding area far from any city or village. Here will be a great discovery of energy in the northeast of Africa. Greed will spread around the world. But it will start a war, and many thousands will be killed because of it. Without the discovery secured, man will destroy each other over its riches. We then stood atop a mountain. The ground would shake; the sky turned dark. Then the mountain exploded in eruption. Extreme weather as the earth has never seen. But for a time of repentance, the weather shall calm, but only for a season. As the oil is removed from the earth that works with other aspects of God's planet, the extreme weather and earthquakes will continue their increase, and parts of the world, as we know today, will become extinct. They will no longer exist. I write down what I am told and what I have seen by the Holy Spirit. I do not reason out in the flesh. I pray for discernment in the prophetic for those visions I am shown.

And there I stood in a city street, people everywhere walking. What appeared to be normal. In the next moment, I could see inside their chest. Their lungs were on fire, burning from the pollution. Mothers were holding their children up close to them. Fire rain will fall from the skies from the worst pollution ever created by man. With their lungs on fire, many will die from incurable lung and blood infections. Where fire rain infects those that it falls on, there will be no fire in the antibiotics to fight back. Large cities will be the worst. Stay out of large population areas as this is the evil from hell that comes to plague mankind. And then the vision ended.

I find myself wanting to sit and think about what I am doing. Reality is work to be done, grass to mow, the daily life of living around me. But here I am before the altar, ordained and ordered by God. I sit here wearing my sackcloth wrapped around my body. My prayer shawl draped over that, the shofar laying as ordered by God against the altar. And my 'Moses Stick' laying before me. Often I've had to use it to pull myself up. My legs are unsteady as I have tried to stand after the visions. Wisdom from Heaven had to teach me there was no room for weakness or reasoning of flesh. If I'd listened to my flesh, or allowed myself to be ruled by my emotions, this day would never have been. Feed your spirit, my friends; you have a Heavenly Father that is calling out to you.

AND THE LORD ANSWERED me, and said, Write the vision, and make it plain upon tables, that he may run that readeth it.~ Habakkuk 2:2

I CAN'T EVEN COUNT the number of conversations, lectures, or speakers I've heard about whether angels existed. It would be early on that I would discern about sharing the intervention of God in my life. Be prepared, for the conversation may not be what you want to hear. Understand the scripture of sewing your pearls before swine.

Do not give what is holy to the dogs; nor cast your pearls before swine, lest they trample them under their feet, and turn and tear you in pieces. ~ Matthew 7:6

Thank you, Lord, for my gift of discernment, trust in the Lord to provide you with what you need.

My Father had been preparing me; He was about to take me deeper into our relationship. There was to begin an outpouring of the prophetic more powerful than anything I could've ever imagined. Beyond all, I could even try to reason, which becomes impossible for the flesh to understand. Again, this is why this was to be a revelation for only my family and my generations to come. Until God would use others to confirm to me the releasing of my experiences, sharing revelations to come.

AND IT SHALL COME TO pass in the last days, saith God, I will pour out of my Spirit upon all flesh: and your sons and your daughters shall prophesy, and your young men shake see visions, and your old men shall dream dreams: And on my servants and on my handmaidens I will pour out in those days of my Spirit; and they shall prophesy: ~ Acts 2:17-18

Chapter 8

Glory Of God

That Friday evening, I had some great fellowship with a pastor that had come into my life. He was a great messenger sent by God. Together that night we shared prayer and fellowship before our Heavenly Father. Truly a blessing for these special times ordained by God Almighty.

Man the Creator

I am standing in the middle of a beautiful lush meadow with an angel. The grass is green, the flowers in full bloom. It must be spring from the look of the blooms. The cattle are feeding out in the grass. The animals move towards us like pets to be petted. Such a beautiful place, so clean and the air smells so fresh. With the blink of an eye, I was moved into a dark, musky smelling, stagnated place. The awful filth I saw as I looked around. Animals just standing there or at least what I thought were animals. What looked like cows, some crippled with legs deformed with hips that appeared to be dislocated or mangled. What was this poor creature animal supposed to be? Imagine a cow's face with a mutant type of disfigurement where the entire face was utterly distorted from what a normal cow looks like.

"What are these pitiful animals?" I asked.

Looking over at the angel, I could hear grunting noises coming from another disfigured type of creature. Its body was extremely fat. Its legs weren't in proportion to its body. What was a face area was totally distorted. It kind of looked like a pig that couldn't even move. Other animals so deformed I couldn't even tell what they were supposed to be.

"What are these?" I shouted out.

How awful for an animal to be so deformed. There were animals squatty and round with feathers and a beak that looked like a chicken. Round and fat with almost no legs. But it couldn't move as a chicken does.

Again I asked, *"What are these poor animals?"*

And the angel began to speak. *"This is what man creates when he tries to be like God in his world, what man has done to that which was made perfect for man. Man is not God, in man's wisdom, he shall never be like God. This is man's creation to feed the people, for money the people of the world will eat. Man, in his wisdom, will never trust that God would provide to feed them all. At what price to mankind will man sacrifice his own human race for profit? For the greed of money and profit, beware of what man labels as food. Does man not know that changing all that was made perfect to imperfect. The outcome this will have. The effects this will have. Man's own children will suffer the imperfect that man will eat. The children will be born with the abnormalities as those cultivated from the animal's man has created. Man will see many illnesses from their own creations where there will be no cure. From what they have created, man will fall prey to the imperfections in their own creations. This will be by man's creation, not from God."*

This I saw, and it's what man and his greed will do. There before my eyes, I saw children deformed in ways that I never knew possible. I saw children moving as if there was a loss of motor skills. I witnessed the population infected by viruses brought on by the foods created by man.

I began to cry. *"Oh Lord, why is this happening, you can't allow man to do this?"*

Again the Spirit of the Lord began to speak, *"There can only be one Creator. So mankind will cry, but man will have turned himself away from that which was sacred. But man still won't care, for what value does man put on the birth of an infant. The children will suffer. Made perfect in the beginning, I have watched man's heart grow darker on the inside. So man shall bring down the wrath of God. For tears and suffering has already begun."*

I woke up thinking about what I had just seen. The suffering has already begun; how and what did that mean? I think I've had enough. My heart was crying on the inside. How would man out of greed inflict such affliction and hardships upon the people of the earth over food?

FOR THE WICKED BOASTS of his heart's desire; He blesses the greedy and renounces the Lord. ~ Psalms 10:3

AS I SAT THERE IN PRAYER before the altar, I began to realize how the Holy Spirit was lifting me up. I prayed for the Holy Ghost to give me strength, both physically and emotionally, in what I was seeing. I knew I had to stay in prayer and not to allow my flesh to pull me away from what I was experiencing in the spiritual realm of God, as I fought back an overwhelming amount of tears. I could feel an incredible move of the Holy Spirit around me every time I was shown a prophetic vision. I had cut a stack of cedar logs so I had plenty to burn through the night. I had laid an old hand-braided rug from the 1800s in front of the fire to kneel upon for prayer. Which worked out great for staying off of the damp ground. The Lord knew, too, I would need my 'Moses Stick.' The supernatural strength was able to help me to my feet. I had no idea what to expect for the evening. The Lord was guiding me, yes humble yourself before the Lord. As I was receiving the Glory of God by my obedience as I prayed by the altar that night, God had instructed me what to do next. I prayed for self-discipline on my part in maintaining the flame, staying in prayer, and not getting sidetracked. I am not a religious person. During this time, I was divinely led by the Holy Spirit to regard the altar and the surroundings as a place of holiness and was not open to having a parade of folks around. This was a time the Lord had ordained some 20 years before. When His had commanded me about the altar's construction. I must insert here too, that I knew this was very old testament with what I was doing. It was not up to man or anybody else to prove or disapprove of what I was to do. This time was ordained by God.

AND I HEARD THE VOICE of the Lord saying, "Whom shall I send, and who will go for us?" Then I said, "Here am I! Send me."~Isaiah 6:8

AS THE NIGHT AIR GREW damper and cooler. I wrapped in a blanket and continued in prayer. Praying to the Lord for interpretation of what I'd already seen. I knew I would journalize in the coming weeks when this had ended. I prayed to the Lord to give me a super ability to recall the visions I'd seen before. I would again be taken and shown more of which was to come. An angel appeared as I was standing before the altar. I could feel a great commotion going on around me, and in the commotion, there was water with waves rolling across a strip of land. It was all around me. The land was completely covered with water. The sky was very dark with thunder clouds. I felt the ground beneath my feet, trembling, and shaking. The ground was emitting a rumbling noise. In the next moment, I am standing atop a mountain looking down at the water covering the land. The only light was coming from the forest that was burning. What I was seeing were flames shooting from the trees, but the trees themselves were not actually burning. How could the forest be burning under the water? How could that be? As I watched the angel, the water began to move away, and there beneath the water lay many people. Some I take were dead. Others were crying in misery. There was such a great presence of suffering, misery, and desolation. Such an awful scene of devastation. I didn't want to see any more. I felt as if I was panicking from what I was seeing. My flesh was battling to take over.

The Spirit of the Lord began to speak, "*There would be disaster after disaster and misery to follow. The clouds will open up, and the earth will roll as natural disasters worse than ever seen in mans' time will fall. Until man cries out and God is all they have. The weather calamities will bring hardships over, over, over again.*"

IF MY PEOPLE, WHICH are called by my name, shall humble themselves, and pray, and seek my face, and turn from their wicked ways; then will I hear from heaven, and will forgive their sin, and will heal their land." ~ 2 Chronicles 7:14

I CAME OUT OF MY PRAYER. If the Holy Spirit hadn't been around me the way He was, I was to the point of disobedience. I was going to stop all of this. I didn't want to hear or see any more. Why show me this? What does it all mean? My body had begun to ache. My rest came only from my prayer. I couldn't think about anything else. I began to doze off in prayer as I laid at the foot of the altar when the Spirit of the Lord called out again. I stood above the destruction looking at a disaster. I was witnessing human nature at its worst. I was seeing the mistreatment of people. People were hostile, and the animals were starving. People were fighting for anything to eat, for their survival. Had man's heart become so full of hate and violence,

"*What was this?*" I asked.

In the next moment, I was standing in a large stadium packed with thousands upon thousands of people. And the angel of the Lord pointed to a small group gathered within them all. We were standing in front of this small group of people out of all the thousands that were there. They were joining hands; they were different. We listened as they prayed, and the angel of the Lord looked over at me and spoke,

"*Out of such disaster, and there is only this remnant of people joining hands and going to the Lord in prayer.*" And the angel continued, "*So many chances have mankind been given and so much has man turned away from. Man could have more wisdom and knowledge of the answers for all his problems, but man has failed. Man shall be given a chance for redemption to return to His Heavenly Father. To show love and obedience to the Father before the Son of Man returns. There will be no less judgment that will come against those that have known the Father and have turned away. Man's final disobedience will be man's worse. And it will lead to his own destruction.*"

And the angel was gone. When I came to, I was lying on the rug before the altar. I must've been crying in my Spirit. Would man finally use his nuclear weapons for the total destruction of people and countries? I was drowning in my empathy of emotion, my feelings for mankind, and what we'd become in the world we lived in. Thinking back, the only thing I could think of was a father's genuine love for his disobedient children. How pure the Lord's love for His children. And here the Lord was showing me that man would have another chance to come to know Him as their Lord and Savior Jesus Christ. Before His return, man would be given the last opportunity to come to the Father before disasters of Biblical proportion would begin to devastate and destroy what God had made perfect. Looking back, I cannot even begin to sum up the emotion and how I was feeling. At this point, I was very much mentally and physically challenged and wanted to end this. What was the purpose of all of this? Praise God that I had a loving family that stood by me through all of this.

Thank you, Lord.

Looking around the morning sky as the sun pushed the darkness away. My thoughts again consumed by what I'd been shown. It reminded me that this is the same way the light from the Word of God pushes the darkness of evil out of man's life. The way I obediently fed the altar fire with the cedar logs that were dried and ready to burn, is the same with God's word. His word is filled with knowledge and wisdom and will give you the strength to prepare for the battles ahead. We must keep our fire burning on the inside by feasting on God's word daily. It is our spiritual food. It is through our daily obedience that you will discover the treasures in God's Word.

BUT HE SAID, "MORE than that, blessed are those who hear the word of God and keep it!"~ Luke 11:27

IN YOUR RELATIONSHIP with Christ, you're better prepared for anything that man and this world could create or devise, to bring down your faith. Rejoice in your victory in your walk with Jesus Christ. You have a Heavenly Father that loves you.

For a few seconds that morning, my thoughts were taken back by my flesh. My body was aching from fighting the flesh. I placed a couple more logs on the fire as the morning breeze blew, and as the Holy Spirit began to come over me. Kneeling down, I took my prayer shawl, pulling it up over my head, and quickly the Holy Spirit slammed into me. This was not an easing or a touch. It was a pick you up off your feet move of the Spirit. I could feel my entire body being taken over by the Holy Spirit. The Kingdom of God is so powerful and yet so very loving. I want you to learn to cherish and just bathe in the Spirit of the Lord when this happens to you. This is pure emotion, the feelings that I felt throughout all of this. In the next seconds, I was standing outside a city gate. The tall man-made walls of stone reaching far above my head. I could see the city gatekeeper as I looked at the very top. I turned around to a large gathering of people, and there before them stood a woman. She was crying, and she was the one the crowd had gathered for. As she stood before the crowd crying

I saw they each had many stones in their hands. Men, women, and even children were standing in front of the crowd. Their little hands wrapped around the large stones. The crowd was ready to stone this pitiful soul to death. By now, their anger was worked up into a rage. And at that moment, Heaven opened up. And this woman about to be stoned was lifted out of harm's way. I turned to face the crowd and they were gone. In the next second, I was standing in a living room. There in front of me was a group of kids playing a video game. The more I watched, the more violent the game was becoming. With splashes of red blood simulated across the screen. The screams of the game characters screaming in terror. Watching, I saw a game that simulated theft, murder, killings, rape. Why do I see this? And in that moment of standing there, I was now standing on the front porch. The boys were leaving, walking down the sidewalk. There lying beside the sidewalk was what appeared to be a hurt cat. The boys instantly kicked the cat sending it into the air. The joy and laughter in their wild hate for what they had done. Shaking my head in disgust, thinking surely not all people were full of such hate or were they? I thought, such an evil spirit, to harm anything or anybody. Was the cat a symbol, what did it mean? In the next moments, I'm standing on a street corner watching this group of young people gathering together. Almost instantly, as I watched in those seconds, shots rang out, and they started laughing. There lying on the ground was what appeared to be a homeless person that had obviously just been shot. Again laughter came from the crowd as they cheered the shooters on. My eyes began to burn as I could feel tears coming down my cheeks for what I had just witnessed. As the crowd moves away, the cat comes walking up to the person that had been shot and begins licking the person. I'm looking at the person lying on the ground and the cat. The body begins to move; they were not dead. I see an angel raise up from the body, a large warrior type angel rising above the ground. Then the angel of the Lord rose up, there was this deafening sound, and the angel pointed to the crowd. Now I began to see demonic spirits that surrounded the crowd. Then time stood still as I heard the loud blast of what sounded like a shofar. An incredibly loud thundering noise was roaring across the air. The angel looked upward, and I began to watch as the demonic spirits began to attack each other as if clawing at each other. Climbing on the next one trying to get away from what was happening. There appearing in an aurora of light, I saw the Warrior angel again. A Warrior from Heaven adorned in Kingdom Glory. The authority of God sent down to destroy these demons that had taken over these kids. He was an army of one, for lack of any other way to describe it. I watched as if the demonic spirits were just dissolving away in those seconds. The energy, the sheer authority, gave witness that God was clearly in charge. Such lawlessness is falling upon the people.

THE SON OF MAN WILL send out His angels, and they will gather out of His kingdom all things that offend, and those who practice lawlessness, ~Matthew 13:41

AGAIN I STRUGGLE WITH words in describing what I had just witnessed. I reached for my blanket as I laid back, thinking about what I had just seen. I began to see how a society with no fear of God and had little reverence for anything good. How could things become so cold, so mean, to other people and animals? Could it be that with so much media today in everyday society that people are desensitizing from the evil before their eyes? That the violence has caused man's heart to grow even darker, as in the days of Noah. Was this the Spirit of Antichrist already working his agenda to turn the world into chaos.

There was no fear in what happened to the crowd for shooting the man. Modern media is used to capturing the minds of our youth. Raised on blood and gore in video games. Neighborhoods in decay with drugs and killings. The criminally insane are becoming more and more violent. We can't be naive about how important your children's souls will be. To be used by the Spirit of Antichrist. As populations of people turn away from Christ, will their sense of hope be gone? To the point of no consequences from a tolerant society where anything goes. Pay attention to violence in all forms of media. They can only see it so much. Before, as a society, you become desensitized to the everyday violence you see on TV. Anywhere a foothold can be taken. I fear the Spirit of Antichrist will use it to attack your children and your family. In Christ, you have the full armor of God to go into battle with. Call it out and claim victory over your children and family in the name of Jesus Christ.

BUT AS THE DAYS OF Noah were, so also will the coming of the Son of Man be.~ Matthew 24:37

Put on the whole armor of God, that you may be able to stand against the wiles of the devil.~ Ephesians 6:11

MY MIND CLEARED AS I looked at things around me. I began to feel the brightness of the light of Heaven and the presence of the Spirit around me. The Holy Spirit telling me I'd shown obedience over the days before. The struggle of my flesh dead from my complete surrender to the power of the Almighty. The Holy Spirit began to give me a renewing, a Holy rejuvenation of His Spirit that would flow forth and touch and nourish the remnant of God's people that were still remaining. The presence of the Spirit of God, my eyes burning, my body is given over to the Spirit. My hands reaching up to touch the heavens. I pulled my hands back to pray, crossing my chest. I could feel my body and control given over, surrendering to the Holy Spirit. It was the evening of the third day. There was no more track of time. What is time to our Heavenly Father?

BUT, BELOVED, DO NOT forget this one thing, that with the Lord one day is as a thousand years, and a thousand years as one day.~ 2 Peter 3:8

THE EVIL OF MAN'S HEART

There I stood in a round room. It's walls made of mud and straw. A woman was lying on a blanket. Several other women were kneeling around her. Her legs were spread apart as she was preparing to give birth. The woman was murmuring a soft chant. As they gathered around her, a scream let out in the chanting; I could make out the cry of a baby. And at the same moment, the cry had stopped. There was a silence that came over the woman. One of the women took a towel and wrapped the baby's dead body. One of the women removed the instrument that had been used to end the baby's life. I walked out of the room. What had I just seen? I wondered, why would I be shown this? This beautiful gift from God, screaming, and then the baby's life brought to an end. I looked over into the direction of my angel, and he looked up. In doing so, I saw a demonic being dancing and rejoicing over the death of the newborn baby. "What is this?" I said to the angel. In that next moment, I was standing in a modern hospital. In an examining room where a woman was lying on the table. There gathered around her were several nurses, All assisting the doctor. I was witnessing the exact same thing happening all over again. The killing of another baby. The taking of human life.

"*Is this an abortion clinic, no this isn't, right,?*" I shouted.

I looked at the angel of God. He began to speak. "*The darkness of man's heart rules his own selfishness in those dead babies and the many yet to be born. Man is destroying thousands of infants every year. As it was in the days of sacrifice to Baal, so it is today. Man is destroying the greatest gift God has given him. With the Spirit of Antichrist increasing, so will the killing of unborn babies increase. When a man can no longer respect the gift of life when birthed from his Heavenly Father, can a man be expected to have reverence for anything else that is Holy? Is not the very gift of birth but a blessing sent from the Father? As in the days of pagan ways, so will their ways of cruelty begin to take over. So then is the gateway of evil that man calls to enter. Can a man believe this type of behavior can be allowed to continue? Is man so stupid to not think the unborn baby has not already been with the Father? That the gift of life has already been blessed with wisdom whom the Father has already breathed life into. Again man's selfish ways will bring about his own destruction.*"

"BEFORE I FORMED YOU in the womb I knew you; Before you were born I sanctified you; ~ Jeremiah 1:5

HOW NAUSEATED I WAS feeling. "*Angel, how can I feel this way if I am here in Spirit?*" I asked.

The angel replies, "*Your Spirit is still linked to your fleshly body until your soul has departed your flesh at death. These are still human emotions that you would feel on your body both physically and emotionally. This is why your physical body has struggled with discomfort after your many returns."*

I just looked and didn't say a word. And in the next second, I stood in a vast open desert as far as I could see with sand beneath my feet. I looked over at the angel, as we turned around, the sand began turning into people. For every speck of sand that covered the desert, there a person was standing.

The angel of the Lord again began to speak. *"That one there would have been a great leader of mankind, that one there a great teacher. That one there held the cure for some of the man's worse diseases. But as man has decided that he knows best. It will again be the choice of self that controls man and his decisions. So has the darkness of death overtaken all the good of what is meant for man's greatest gift, the gift of life. Today they continue to kill millions of unborn infants, and for this, they will be judged. The day will come when the unborn shall rise. So sad how a man could have so much, But destroys the very living soul of those that would have been born to bring about man's greatest discoveries. Such destruction that man has inflicted on his self."* The angel of the Lord looked over at me. I was very weak.

In the distance, I could hear drums. I could hear singing, almost like a pounding movement of an army. There was an echo that filled the sky. Again and again, as if in harmony were these echoes. The people that were standing had changed back to grains of sand. The loud echoing kept growing louder and louder, thundering across the Heavens. There in the distances, I could begin to see motion. The closer it came, the larger it was. As if the land was moving, the body of land was moving for as far as I could see. It was like a huge wave approaching. The air I was breathing was warm and full of the Spirit of the Lord. The angel of the Lord pointed over.

I said, *"What is this that spans further than my eyes can see?"*

The angel of the Lord replies, *"This is the Lord's Army. It moves even closer as that time nears. They are gathering. The Lord is preparing for His return. The evil that has walked with a man*

will come to its end. For a man has killed the unborn, so has man cursed his own existence. Where people could gather for fun and praise of their Heavenly Father. They will only gather to mourn their own dead, still living soul. A soul that will know no rest. A soul that will crave anything to bring it peace. There will be no peace to be found. Man's addiction will only continue to grow. Man's cravings will rule a man's mind. Man will want to hide in his own shame as his cravings take over. How can man's ways be so depraved to do what they have done to each other and the newborn birthed by their Heavenly Father? How can evil man expect to find harmony with each other when his heart is so darkened to take another human's life without regard to others. Therefore, man's heart has become afflicted and so tormented by his world around him. With that which is yet to come, Man will destroy each other, blaming others for their destruction of life. Those that once knew the Father have long departed. They are full of self, kings in their own flesh they rule over. Oh, how many have known the truth. Yet they fight like animals over things of the world, that are dead to the God of Heaven. So shall it be that man's mind shall turn against him? All things that are not of God shall rule his life? For with their Heavenly Father, they would have had their peace. That time is approaching when it will be gone. The attacks of the Antichrist will only grow stronger against man's mind. Without the Heavenly Father, their minds will not be able to war off the attacks to come. Their minds will battle reasoning as they watch their own destruction. And such is the evil of man. Man will only numb his pain as that which is not of the Lord will come to torment him even more." And then the angel was gone.

My eyes staring into the flames of the altar fire with tears streaming down my cheeks. I lay on the ground too weak to stand. My entire body was limp before the Holy Spirit of the Lord. I could not move my physical body consumed by the Fires of Heaven. Trying to write this out, I couldn't stop asking myself. *"What has man done?"* So many people that had so much to offer to the civilization of man being destroyed by man's dark heart. Was this the evil that walks with a man, controlling the destiny of him as foretold in the scriptures of that which is to come. All destroyed to bring about the ultimate purpose of God as told in the bible. God knew what man would become.

The Holy Spirit has told me to insert this vision I was shown recently here. It is not mine to question. But to only do, as instructed. I've learned to show obedience when instructed from above.

FOR PROPHECY NEVER came by the will of man, but holy men of God spoke as they were moved by the Holy Spirit. ~ 2Peter 1:21

AND WHEN THE ANGEL of the Lord appeared, we were standing up from a large group of people. There were 32 world leaders gathering in a circle, and they were holding hands and praying. Some were crying out, looking upwards to the sky. An angel of the Lord appeared above them, and in his hand, he held a large conical shaped horn, and when he blew the horn, the power of God came out falling upon those in the circle. These will be the nations that turned away from Israel. And now cry out for forgiveness for what they had become. Pagan nations where God was taken out of everything once good. And there was nothing of God to be found. A thundering trumpet that blasted across lands then all was destroyed in seconds their country, the lands, the people, all were killed. There was no more crying out from these places. Their lands were silent. Where the 32 had stood, there were 12 Angels holding swords pulled pointing towards the heavens. And, I saw when I had awakened a new time when peace had come across the earth. What did I see?

BE STILL, AND KNOW that I am God; I will be exalted among the nations, I will be exalted in the earth! ~Psalms 46:11

Chapter 9

The Lord Is Your Strength

My thoughts on what I'd been shown had utterly consumed me. It wasn't about who I am. I'm still asking, "Why me?" It was about Jesus Christ and the things that are to come. I've had to move past what people may think or say. Never let the world make you forget; it's between you and God, and no one else. Mentally I was as sharp and alert as when I had started three days before. Physically my body was drained. Describing the supernatural of the Heavens just goes beyond words. In gathering my thoughts on what all I've been shown, has mankind grown so full of hate that the only outcome is complete self-destruction? Friends, we can't fall to the weakness of the world, where we only think the evil of man is destroying all that was good. If we do then why would people even want to trust and believe in God when there is so much negativity? We need to stop this mindset. Praise God that Jesus Christ gives us the hope we need to see this world through to the end. Again it would only be at the calling of the Holy Spirit and my peace in Christ that you are reading this today. If there should be a hidden nugget in what God has shown me I pray it'll be to help mankind prepare spiritually for what this world is becoming, and that this testimony will serve as a message to folks in building up your faith and that of your family's. This world is transforming and unfortunately it's not all good. You have to understand that finding love and peace can only come through Jesus Christ. After the revelations I've seen, I know the events that are taking place in this big world around us are going to bring about the fulfillment of the book of Revelations. Wars and rumors of wars are on the news before you every day. The realization of the scriptures is happening, it doesn't matter whether it's the evening news or on the internet. Friends again, God never promised that your life would be easy. But he did promise that he would always be by our side, and his son's sacrifice for us regardless of what we would face would be more than enough to get through. Prophetic events are coming into alignment with scripture, and we must continue to look and seek that relationship with Christ. Our Heavenly Father has an incredible homecoming stored up for us in Heaven. Do not fear this world you are in today. Trust in God with the journey we must all make, it's your life, your pilgrimage. Learn to be led in the dark by listening to that still small voice. We aren't talking about a new wind blowing here. We are talking about blind faith. Blind faith is the blessing given to man by Jesus Christ. Blind faith is where you find how much strength in Christ you have. Your Heavenly Father's gift in your walk with Him, those special moments when you know only God could have done that, trust Him.

FOR THE JOY OF THE Lord is your strength.~ Nehemiah 8:10

THESE PROPHETIC REVELATIONS of world events that are coming will test the very foundations of faith inside the hearts of people. It's not just about man and his religious views but about a man and his relationship and intimacy with God. Take the religion out of your relationship with God and move closer to the Father as He wraps His arms around His children. I only know that I've seen Prophetic events that are to happen, that I didn't ask to see or experience. But with that evil, I've also seen many good things to come as well. Satan uses the darkness of confusion and pain in a fallen world to make man look and focus on the misery, the worst, and the darkest. Unfortunately, It's what man's flesh can concentrate on the easiest, but you will find nothing of God in it. You must teach yourself to focus on the good, my friends, because that is where you will find the goodness of Christ dwells. God is all around us, amen.

FINALLY, BRETHREN, whatsoever things are true, whatsoever things are honest, whatsoever things are just, whatsoever things are pure, whatsoever things are lovely, whatsoever things are of good report; if there be any virtue, and if there be any praise, think on these things.~ Phillippians 4:8

OVER THE DAYS, WEEK's, months to come in your life write down what you hear from God. You'll be lifted up in the very word that God will give you. Then go back and reread what you've written down, explore the revelation in the word God gives you. Man can't control the move of God; you'll hear people say that man shut down the movement of God in their church service. I just roll laughing on that. Look at everything in this big world and who the Great Creator is. Man's self thinks the move of God can be shut down, but friends, then God, was never there, and your emotion was dictating those circumstances.

"*Oh, I am coming to my children, the time draws near,*" the Lord cries out. When the Lord calls out it usually means that there will be a prophetic blessing soon to be shown to me. Today, I've learned to call it a blessing and no longer a curse. We must look for the unveiling from the Kingdom. Nothing you can do has control over the Holy Spirit. The Holy Spirit has the Kingdom authority to touch your spirit man at any time. So never mind how bad your bad-self might be; your legs will bend. Let's just make sure this is good and clear, God can and will use whomsoever He deems necessary.

Over the years, I've learned how tough the move of the Holy Spirit and the power of the Lord can be on my flesh and my physical body. It is the greatness of God almighty, that has sustained me. It's just that powerful. In the early years, honestly, I wasn't sure how to withstand it. In the spiritual world, I learned to handle the pull on my flesh. I know it's during those times that Jesus Christ wrapped me in His arms. Some of my pastor friends have said I have the gifting of a Leviticus Priest because of what happens. I share that comment, not as a boast or to make a prideful statement. But a comment to help you to understand further this burden of the Lord that I've carried for so many years. It's not about me. We are a vessel being used by our most High God. For a long time, especially in the early years there were few people I could share with. I learned early on that when I did share, they had to be very grounded in who they were in Christ. The human emotions controlled by the flesh can really rear its ugly self, so I've only shared when specifically instructed by the Lord, period. And for so many years, I showed obedience when called. I know today it was deep calling to deep.

The attacks on children will be in ways never seen before in history. Are you prepared for the spiritual battle to come? In Christ Jesus, I pray that you are. There is so much coming at the children, trying to capture their minds.

BUT WHOSO SHALL OFFEND one of these little ones which believe in me, it were better for him that a millstone were hanged about his neck, and that he were drowned in the depth of the sea.~ Matthew 18:6

SOLDIER, YOU MUST PRAY and be ready to confront that evil when it shows itself. Once someone said to me, it's always been the same in every generation and that the older ones worry themselves. Friends, as I've stated before, have you ever seen the world so confused as it is today? The Spirit of Division is like a runaway train, tearing apart anything that gets in its way. It's coming, and it's coming hard and fast in every part of society. We live in violent times, and the growing calamity of violence increases by the hour. The spirit of Antichrist wants to steal our freedom. The freedom of our minds.

AND BE NOT CONFORMED to this world: but be ye transformed by the renewing of your mind, that ye may prove what is that good, and acceptable, and perfect, will of God.~ Romans 12:2

THE SPIRIT OF ANTICHRIST can advance domestic calamity against all nations and all people. How is the spirit of Antichrist being perpetrated against our families? When was the last time you were really upset over a major crime you have seen on the news? A murder, a killing of a fellow human being as you watched TV. I believe your last comment might have been, wasn't that awful or how sad. And then you went back to eating or reading the paper. People are becoming more and more desensitized to blood and evil. The gore on the news is just another killing. Movies are all about killing after killing, and I know it's just a movie. Child trafficking and the destruction of their lives, controlled by the evil of this world. Friends, is this a natural behavior for children of Christ not to care? Not to step up on behalf of your family. Look at it through your Spiritual eyes. Evil is shuffling the cards for the souls of our children. You will learn there are many jobs in the Army of the Lord. Is God calling you to be a Warrior? Well, your time is here.

Take Away the Compassion

As I stood there beside the angel in a home. All looked normal in the flesh. But in the spiritual, the angel began to show me TV's, not one but one in every room. And there before each person, they sat staring into the box as if hypnotized by what they were watching. In the spiritual, it was like a box cover with almost a cobweb appearance encasing the TV. Again what was right and meant for family entertainment had become deceptive and mind-controlled programming. The angel pointed towards the TV and as I looked I began to see something I had never seen before. The only way I know how to describe what I was seeing is that it was in a type of 3D mode. I was looking beyond the standard picture on the TV. I was able to see demon-like beings in another dimension behind the images. They were doing things to control the flesh of the people watching from the other side. Almost like a form of spiritual mind control. I can only describe what I was seeing to assist you in being able to visualize what was before me. Again what was I seeing? At that moment, the TV box surely had spiritual control over the flesh. In a second the TV went out, it was dark.

The angel said, "*Watch.*"

Immediately the children began to scream, upset that the TV was off. The more the mother worked on the TV, the more the children screamed and started getting upset and confusion set in. Once the TV was on, the calamity had calmed down. In another room, a man stood in front of his TV watching a game. The TV went off. The man began to act as the children and mimic the same behavior because the TV was off. The amount of control our TV has over us, unfortunately, has made us become that dependent on them. I am so guilty.

Then the angel began to speak. "*The control of information that is given out over our TV and computer will have enough control to usher in the spirit of Antichrist beginning with the children. The indoctrination and desensitizing of children will allow for those things that are dark and evil to be portrayed as good and clean. Man will become easily deceived by that which will be put before his eyes. Today this is already influencing and controlling his thoughts. As the lights flick-*

ered on the TV, everything was bright and beautiful and eye-catching appeal to the fleshly nature that makes man his weakest. Hypnotizing music to keep your attention. Oh, my children, you feed on all the wrong things, and then you wonder why. Can the violence and the unclean before your eyes be good for the children?"

I didn't want to write this in here, but I'm as guilty as any and all out there when it comes to the media. I have realized that I too had been blinded by that of a spirit of Antichrist. Spoonfed by programming that has no concern about what is right and decent for our families. Don't think it's too late to take it back and make that which is dark and evil clean. God is still in charge, and we, the Warriors for Christ, can make the right changes. Souls can yet be saved.

Perfection Man's Way

Again I was taken away by the angel. I walked down a corridor in a very nice hospital. We are standing in a nursery area next to what looks like a large laboratory. Something is just different. See, I am standing in a corporate baby factory. Things are changing, and today it's more acceptable to custom order that baby made to your specifications for 'Perfection'. These are designer babies. Striving to reach perfection as brainwashed by the media and make-belief imagery of perfection. By now, generations have already been bombarded by all that is perfect in the flesh is good. With more and more problems with infertility in the future. The growth in sperm banks and catalog shopping for a baby becomes more commonplace if you have the money. Man has learned they can replace what God has given as a natural way to have children. To mail ordering babies for perfection. The flesh is ruling, demanding that these parents have the perfect child with perfect genetics for height, build, and intelligence. The nurse walks away with your paperwork. See, your genes are tested for defects. Made perfect to fit that part of a society where all is made perfect. As parents strive for their perfection to fit into a society based on the lust of the flesh, they seek out perfection. With the end results from a child that will hopefully excel in a society of Antichrist where perfection is not only socially expected, but a must in this age of self. Perfection for healthy parents will be brought together under government standards and guidelines for sperm banks. Where God can no longer be God. Where God is no longer needed.

See, this is the future for those that will handle conception on their own. You think this helps people to become parents. How wonderful to be blessed with a baby, you think. See, by this time, nutrition, environmental contaminants, and air quality have made 75% of the population sterile. Early government sterilization programs have been very effective in controlling undesirable, uncontrollable populations which, has proven to be a cheaper way of handling populations. The spirit of Antichrist knows it's better to eliminate a population instead of worrying about feeding them. And the cost of health care. Well, that's a burden this world can't afford. Where it's normal to have assistance with fertility drugs and modern medical procedures for conception. In this hard-hearted future, people will say why would a loving God do this to me. Make me unable to have children? By now, God is the blame for everything. God becomes the greatest excuse for the spirit of Antichrist to take over. It won't be about the opportunity to adopt. That won't matter. There will be no room for an imperfect child. A society governed by a spirit of Antichrist will 'Label' these loving children, a gift from God to be imperfections. And, they will be looked upon as a burden to a family's productivity. See, unfortunately, from the early years of society from substance abuse and pollution in the world, mental issues have caught up with the population that is being born naturally. Even in the laboratory, careful screening has to take place to prevent further disorders from happening. It will become much worse as this part of the population is a burden on the government entitlement programs. Mental disorders labeled and institutionalized. Look for the categorizing and labeling of children to occur more than ever. Futures planned out and managed by the government. Everyone must be productive in society, or they're a non-contributor. This is the spirit of Antichrist. This is the future where God and morality have been removed.

In this world, the spirit of Antichrist has determined; unfortunately, there is no room for the elderly. Respect is gone, honor thy mother and father are politically wrong. Taking care of the widows and children, as written in the Bible, no longer applies. They're just more drains on government and society, and caring for them has grown cold, insensitive, and this hardness gives little reverence to what life the elderly have remaining. Many of the elderly that still have their faith, waiting for the return of Jesus Christ, face incredible hardships. Due to living conditions and health care, many have fallen through the system. Struggling to live lives with families or friends. Hidden from government oversight. See, in this age and time, if you're not productive for the state, then you're a liability that must be dealt with.

The love and compassion we know today will not be the same in the future. Unproductiveness is a social order controlled by government intervention into every walk of daily human life. There will be no room for those individuals in society that are old and no longer contributing to society. Many will be put into government-controlled institutions only to be housed and heavily sedated with, government manufactured drugs. Through government-controlled and owned pharmaceutical companies where huge profits are made all in the name of a better society. A more manageable society. Where all that is evil is that of a spirit of Antichrist. A society where love and compassion have given way to selfish ideology to keep people productive and working. The Antichrist government and world prison system put the populations in bondage. Your choice of euthanasia has become the standard for a quick way out of the suffering and is furnished by the state. Services are held on a regular basis. See, this has become politically correct and will take you to your nirvana. There is no political correctness to please people.

Today that spirit of Antichrist has control and demands how and what society will become. It has become forbidden to say the name, Jesus. This is the end times that is to fall upon man prophesied by the Holy Spirit and what I've been shown. Lord, why must I see these things? Like a pile of snow beside the road. What was white and beautiful is now dirty and has turned to ice — a metaphor for a cold, polluted society. Jesus Christ is the only light of the hope and strength that we have. Seek him and learn to find strength and courage in the word of God. Don't end up in that dirty pile of snow melting away. You are a child of the Almighty God the most High; Your Father is the King of Kings, there is nothing else you need.

In the early years, I would say, why God, why can't I see all the pretty stuff? Like feathers and gold and just feel good things. Once I did ask an angel these exact words. His reply, *"You are a Gatekeeper!"* and I just nodded. Eventually, there would be more to this than I realized.

In The Field of Psychiatric Care

By now, this is becoming unmanageable. The demand for health care in helping people to deal with issues is epidemic, how to cope, the mental distress, and extreme substance abuse is uncontrollable. The Psychiatric community struggles to diagnose and identify what it is they are facing. These attacks are affecting the mental capacity of one out of every three people. And in a society where the spirit of Antichrist rules very little is done. Understand this is playing into the end times. And man really thought they could live life any way they wanted to. Treatment for the demonic attacks is handled with strong medicines and chemical compounds. That will turn the mind and body into nothing more than a Zombie. Cannibalism begins to first appear in society, and the government will blame it on substance abuse. Man blames the drugs and anything else they can come up with. Friends, did you really believe that bath salt would turn a person into a cannibal? Just lies and deception to cover up the unknown. Or I prefer to call it the unseen without your spiritual awareness. In society, animal type behaviors become more and more common afflicting people. Cannibalistic behavior feeds from the demonic world, and it will take over and show up more. It will happen. Know Jesus, my friends, or else! In the early years, the healthcare field began to encounter demonic spirits that had taken over people's minds. But

without Christ and the knowledge and power of the Lord above. The world is becoming defenseless, unfortunately for what will happen in the prophetic. Media doesn't realize they are prophesying the future. Or do they? The fallen angel or devil was angel over what? The airways. In the early years, they labeled it fake news. But we all knew what we really wanted was just the truth. Can you see it happening before your eyes today?

WHEREIN IN TIME PAST ye walked according to the course of this world, according to the prince of the power of the air, the spirit that now worketh in the children of disobedience: ~ Ephesians 2:2

CARING FOR THESE MENTALLY sick individuals is costly, and caring for these mentally ill individuals is unacceptable and expensive to the government. Government control review boards and society institutionalized all people considered not normal. You ask what the future will determine as healthy. Look around today, and what do you call normal. In the future, this will become a harsh part of society. Extensive housing facilities go under construction in far away out of sight locations. See, man doesn't want to be reminded of that part of imperfection in society. When the answers to the entire problem come from one single place, "Jesus!" Keep in mind; your right mind is made right by knowing Jesus as your Lord and Savior. Friends, these will be the end times. They are coming. And the demonic attacks on mankind will be as real and devastating as the burn of fire against your flesh. In the next chapter, living and breathing take on a new meaning.

Chapter 10

The End of The Third Day

I'm tired, and my body is aching. I continue to carry the wood, maintaining the altar's fire. Mentally at this point, I am spent, everything that I am is to the Lord. Praying is my only thought. It is the strength of my God that carries me until the end tonight. In my prayers, I have gone deeper and deeper beyond my practical reasoning that I may have ever had. For surely this night, the Holy Spirit is in command. Spiritually how hard it is to die to our flesh. Without the Holy Spirit and going deeper in our love of Christ, our battle with the flesh is lost. For almost twenty years, I'd been shown this altar. And for those years, I had prayed for God to reveal the revelation of the altar and what it would mean. I prayed at the cross that I had been instructed to put up on the knoll, almost 20 years before. None of it made any sense back then. Have you ever heard the Lord tell you to do something that just seemed so out of the ordinary? You must choose to listen to the Holy Spirit and just trust the Lord. The Lord's way is not our way. So here I humbly stand in awe before a cross and an altar ordained by God Almighty that has come to fulfillment. My eyes fixated on the altar flame. This most beautiful place where I've come dropping to my knees, I began to pray. The presence of the Holy Spirit was so incredibly soothing. My body relaxed, it was as if God Almighty Himself was standing there telling me to blow my Shofar. I reached over for the Shofar that was leaning against the altar, and I began to blow.

The Shofars sound calling out to the heavens echoing back from the distant mountains. It was an extraordinary moment. Almost unable to stand, I placed my Shofar back against the altar. Preparing to kneel in prayer again, I look up. There, an angel appeared and reached out for me. I was so exhausted I don't remember being able to move. A couple of hours would pass before I was able to recollect my time. When I came back to consciousness, I was lying in front of the altar on the rug. My body was aching, struggling to gather my thoughts on what I'd just experienced. I'm at a loss for words to describe what happened next. Understand friends, what you experience in the spirit is different from what your flesh and your mind will try to reason; our flesh is not of the soul. For several moments it was like I couldn't move. It was as if I was standing in the fire, smoke, and flames shooting skyward around me. In the next seconds, I was standing amongst a group of people. I began to cry out, *"Lord, Lord, why have you shown me these things?"* There was a terrible torment and a Spirit of Division washing over the people as I was watching. I don't know what happened. The way I was feeling, all I remember is waking up and gazing into the sky as if looking through a telescope. There was no confusion, and my mind was as clear as could be. I realized the Lord makes no mistakes, and for some reason, HE had shown me what HE wanted me to see.

Moving closer to end times as written in the Bible. We are going to go through unimaginable things. For a lot of people, it'll be really hard on them. Those with a weak faith built on emotionalism and religious ways will struggle. As awful as this may sound, friends, the days of what I have called "**Cotton Candy Jesus**" are over with what is coming down the road for the future. A faith built on emotionalism without intimacy and a knowing relationship of who Jesus Christ is will not suffice. The pride of self will question and squirm and do whatever it takes to sell out to the spirit of Antichrist to preserve themselves, their money, and their families. For these folks, they'll know no difference. It will be life as usual. See, they never had a relationship with Christ for whatever reason, and it won't matter. They choose to take another direction. The clock is ticking down, and soon it will be too late. The demons of hell are about to be unleashed upon all of the people of this earth. It's coming, the gates of hell will open.

Look around you, watch the news, you'll see misery loves good company. Now listen to what I'm telling you. The word *'Remnant'* oh what that word will come to mean in the future. Never forget that word. Because a day approaches, and that will be who you will become. Each of you must take your Intimacy with the Lord and make it very personal. I want you to feel a closeness, as you've never felt before in your walk with the Lord. As the return of the Lord gets closer, this will become very important. I can't overemphasize this enough to you. At the beginning of the end times, you'll know your relationship with Jesus Christ will be the only place to find comfort and peace of mind. With a great emphasis here, on your peace of mind.

Shielded away from torments and confusion going on around you. It has already begun, and the evil that is called good, will take hold of everything with its Antichrist spirit.

AND THE PEACE OF GOD, which surpasses all understanding, will guard your hearts and minds through Christ Jesus.~ Phillippians 4:7

LOOK FOR THE DIVISION that wants to rip apart and separate people from each other; it's called a spirit of division. All this is setting the stage for everything that has an Antichrist spirit about it. Finding that special relationship between you and Jesus Christ will allow you to know what is going on around you. Pray for your gift of discernment; this will help you. It's why God gives us the gifts of the Spirit that he does. Understand this. There will be those of you that will be sought out by others, longing to have your peace and faith and to find out the truth about God's love for His children. This is about the Lord using you and helping others in finding their relationship with Christ. Moving closer to the Father in these end times will also help you to identify the hate around you Spiritually. Your love of Christ and your faith must be strong so that you're able to help others. When they, too, are dealing with their trials and tribulations. Study and understand the word 'Remnant' and how it applies to the followers of Christ because that's what you will become. As the New World Order without Christ is taken over by everything, not of God. You'll be a 'Remnant' of the followers of the 'Way.' Some of you will live to tell of your relationship with Christ Jesus. Unfortunately, many will not. And understand this. Now hear what the Lord commands you. You will be hated by that spirit of Antichrist. Things will change; today you worship freely. In the future, those times will end. The Word of God will take on a new meaning, as will the word 'Outcast.' You must be prepared; you've been warned! As your work will have been ordained from Heaven, this is your ministry, to carry on to save souls in these end times. Friends, we are moving past the 50 flavors of worship. Once upon a time, there was a fast food place that served a hundred different milkshakes. And the last one was called 'Grasshopper.' I always wondered how 'Grasshopper' became the one hundredth flavor. Friends, our goal is not to be the grasshopper. The last in line. God's goal is that you are the 'Crusader,' the head of the line. Pray for your boldness in making that stand in the name of Jesus Christ. Trust in the Lord, and if he gave you the task, then he'll certainly give you what you need to do the job. Don't allow you and your family to become that grasshopper at the end. For you will perish, for you never found your relationship in Christ. Don't allow the world to steal your Jesus. Take a stand and push back. We are children of a mighty and real God. Look around you. You already see the confusion taking hold of every aspect of life in this world. I know many prophetic events are going to take place. Preparing the world for the Lord's return. I've seen this. And anybody reading this that studies their Bible can see the prophetic events coming together. God loves us, and He wants His children prepared. Friends, there is going to be the greatest end-time revival that man has ever seen before the return of Christ. Are you ready?

On the night of the third day, I was in prayer and holding onto my prayer list. I'd taken this list to the altar with me, and prayed over it. Looking back now, years later, many of these people would come to be healed and touched in ways that only God could do. I still have that prayer list with me today. Over my lifetime, I've seen many of God's people come and go from my life. People that were there for only a season, for whatever reason. I just know that season has come and gone. Trust in the Lord He's got this.

Standing by the altar, the angel of the Lord would visit again as I was in prayer. There I was standing beside a great field.

The angel began to tell me. *"Those that work to control the food will be of the spirit of Antichrist. The earth has been blessed to feed all generations after generations of people that are to come."*

I listened as I stood in a field looking. The vegetables were the size of a bush. I had never seen anything like it before. The vegetables so green and brightly colored fruits that were flourishing for as far as my eyes could see. Such a beautiful place. There was water flowing from the grounds. The crops were well-nourished and plentiful from the nutrients in the soil and in the waters that flowed. A man was standing nearby, holding over his head some sort of a snake;

it looked like it was wrapped around his shoulders. Reaching from around his neck, he tossed the snake into the bubbling spring of water, the water stopped. I watched wondering why he would do that. Again he went to another spring of water. And again, the serpent was thrown into the water, and the water stopped. See friends, I was watching that which was full of life and gave life to all things healthy and good began to die. Where I'd once stood in the beautiful field, I now saw vegetables so small, covered with bugs that, for some reason, weren't eating the plants. With each vegetable and fruit harvested from the field, I could see what appeared to be snakes crawling around them. The food looked dead and without life. Then I saw that it was being packaged and shipped off to be eaten by hungry people.

Again the angel spoke and said, "*This is what man has done to control the food. Man will control the waters and destroy the goodness of the food and share it with only those that can pay. Man will have such a selfish heart; he will control populations by controlling their food supply. As areas of desolation grow across the earth, the ground will be unable to grow anything. Many will starve. Again man was seen destroying what was already perfect.*"

I woke up drowning in a bath of emotions, thinking about what I'd just seen. I knew that only God could undo the damages to the earth that have already been done. I began to pray.

I need to insert some thoughts here as I look back. It's been a challenge gathering and organizing my many journal notes to be able to allow you a glimpse into my world and to share what I've experienced. At times I felt like a farmer that has gathered his harvest from the field. Divinely praying for the Holy Spirit to lead me in what would and wouldn't go into this testimony. Some people may read the words, but I pray you'll be able to hear the word as you are reading. For me, getting through a sentence or a paragraph, the Word of God becomes alive. My mind and thoughts are immediately taken away, and I'm shown many things that are yet to come. It may go to where I am replaying something the Lord has shown me, and like an exploding firework, I will have God's Word take me and begin to show me something else. I pray that you could be touched in such a special way. I want to share this with you as another example of God's Word exploding before me. I would be sitting in class at Bethlehem Christian University and while listening to the study. It would be all I could do to follow along because my thoughts and God's Word would carry me away to another time and place. This is our God. Do you want to know HIM? Are you ready for that? Are you prepared to share His Words? Oh, so many underestimate the power and authority that the Word of God has. Is it illusions or visions when you have stood inside a tent and watched the Great Prophet? Or have you stood quietly and watched a gathering that has taken place in a vision God had given you? Knowing the entire time you've never been there and learning that only the authority of God could cause such an encounter to happen. Friends understand this. It's between you and God. I don't want you reasoning, but praying. The Kingdom of God exceeds far beyond reasoning and comprehension.

Man will never begin to grasp the workings of God in this world. You can feel free to contact me to share where God is moving in your life, for we are One in the body of Christ as believers.

My three days and three nights were to come to an end, I was allowing the fire to burn down and would soon put the fire out. I knew I had accomplished what God had called me to do. The Spirit of God and the winds of Heaven had pushed me through. There is still so much more yet to be shared. Where do I stop? It's imperative to mention here again that twenty years before when the Lord had prophetically given me my task for the construction of the altar. In His instructions, I was to collect the purest of the cedar ash from the burnt Cedar Wood. At the time, this made very little sense to me of what I would be doing. Once the altar fire was burning, I was able to witness the miracles of God before my eyes. When my fasting and praying had ended after the three days, I'd collect that most purist cedar ash as instructed. I just looked at it, but I knew God's touch was upon it. So it has been put away. I know when that time comes, God will instruct me what to do with this ash. I've had a few that have offered up insight, and I just smile, for another day will come, as this one has that it was gathered from. God knows.

In thinking back over those three days and nights, I remember that I didn't want to leave the spot where I was. The peace I was feeling from the fellowship with the Lord was like no other. I learned words to describe those special moments didn't matter. The glory of the Lord I had experienced was special enough. I thought if all people could have just a taste, the visions, the smell of the Holy of Holiness that rose from the fire. Would it help them to believe more about how real God is? We have to love and trust God all the way. God will do miracles, and I pray that in God's timing, you too will have your miracles and find intimacy with your Heavenly Father.

I gathered the last of my ash and put it in a jar and secured the lid. I grabbed my bottle of anointing oil. Pulling my prayer shawl from my shoulders covering my head, I stirred the last remnant of ashes. I laid down and began to weep. It was as if someone I loved so much had been there with me. There was an incredible amount of emotion that I was consumed with. But it wasn't sadness; it was happiness, a closeness, a loving, caring love with someone you may have searched your entire life to find. It was in these moments too. I knew that I'd been washed in the blood of Christ. That I, consumed by the Lord's fire, was ordained for this specific time in my life so long ago. God is so faithful. Exhaustion from the three days and nights, along with fasting, had caught up with me. I went into the house. Truly exhausted from my experience with God. My hunger pains begin to set in crying to be fed. After eating and taking a shower. I continue to smell the sweet smell of the altar fire all around me. I went into my bedroom, sitting

on the bed, I looked at my wife. I just shook my head and said, *"Only God could have taken me and shown me the things I have seen, nobody would believe this would they?"*

She just smiled and quietly replied, *"God knows, and God will let those people that HE wants to know, know, get some sleep now."*

The Glory of the Lord is so powerful. I felt like I'd been run over by the Holy Ghost train. Sometime during the night, I knew I had gotten out of bed and looked out the window; it was almost as if I was dreaming. Straining stretching my eyes to see a small tiny ember still burning upon the altar's fire. But there was none to be seen. As I'm standing there looking out, tears began streaming down my cheeks. Even to this day, I struggle to hold back the flow of tears when I think back. Only God, only God Almighty could've set me upon this course of divine destiny. Listen to what I'm confirming to you. Our Heavenly Father is as real as your eyes reading these words. I returned to bed.

BEHOLD, I TELL YOU a mystery: We shall not all sleep, but we shall all be changed.~ 1 Corinthians 15:15

This is a picture of the Cross and the Altar, with my Shofar, the Prayer List and my Moses Stick, that I was divinely instructed by God Almighty to have with me on those three days and nights.

Chapter 11

The Refiner's Fire

I started writing almost immediately after the three days and nights and continued to do so for several days afterward. Once again, I want to remind you and encourage you. When you have heard from God in a dream, a vision, or that quiet small voice, take out your pencil and paper and write. You may not have any idea what it means or what it's about. But in time, God will send you your answer. And please, I know you have a great memory too. But even a great memory gets tired. So write it down. Remember, this is your testimony. Whether the loss of a loved one you miss, the death of a friend or family, a life of alcohol or drug addiction, write it down. Were you homeless, were you incarcerated, has the school of hard knocks been a rough one? Write it down. It is your testimony, and you sharing it with others will allow other people to see how God has worked in your life. Friends, you never know the tribulations people are in or have experienced. Friends, we are all human, and by sharing, you may help to deliver that person or family from the pain or attacks they are under. Over the years, I wrote in my old journal, on pieces of paper, on napkins, anything I could find at the moment, it didn't matter. Just do it.

You're probably wondering with all of this going on. How are you living? Unfortunately, we can't always stay on top of the mountain and I was about to come down into the valley. What I didn't realize was how bad the attacks would come. Many many years before, I had been warned by an angel that the attacks would come. Friends, I had no idea how severe the attacks would be. Don't you ever think the other side doesn't play for keeps. Understand the value of your soul and what it means. I made my living as a contractor. When the economy had begun to collapse in 2008, I was building homes and had projects under construction. But as the economy continued to get worse, money and supplies were dwindling. A home company that I was a distributor for went out of business because of the downturn and left me with a backorder of debt for a large amount of money. They failed to deliver my building materials. On top of that, I was struggling to even get materials from other suppliers to be able to finish the homes under construction. Then things began to spiral out of control like a perfect storm. Unfortunately, I had money on deposit from customers to be used for their projects, but it became harder and harder to make ends meet. creating just an awful situation. I was trying my best to try to complete the jobs. It was a time of life where it went from bad to worse. These were not good times. The attorney told me I should have just shut things down right then and there, but I didn't. I was hoping and praying that I could make things right. I had gone from twenty-two crews working down to one. But the dripping spigot eventually stopped, and I would pay the price. By the time I had shut the business down, my life had become turned upside down. When my construction company went into bankruptcy, I was unable to return the funds for the unfinished projects. Those were days that I neither cared to walk in or even relive. Those were days that the tears and every breath I took, I could feel. The Holy Spirit led me to put all the details of my testimony here. See friends, I know there are many others out there just like me that have been through the trials and tribulations of life. So please again let go of it. And I'll repeat this, don't allow your past to dictate your future. Find your peace in Christ and let the torment of the past go. It doesn't matter what it is, relationships, business, adult children, family. Set yourself free of your misery. If you need a reminder, put up scripture in the kitchen, the bathroom wherever but do it. Nowhere does the Bible promise you a tomorrow, you have to take charge of your life. If you need prayer, write to me, and we shall pray together, Amen? How strong is your flesh? It can be just that strong if not controlled by the Holy Spirit.

One day during this dark time of my life I was in prayer crying out to God, "*Why Lord?*" Now, this wasn't funny at the time, but on this day it was as if the Lord was standing right there beside me. I will never forget it was a beautiful sunny morning and the Lord answered me, "*How can you be a Great Warrior without a great battle, greater your battle sweeter the Victory.*" I cried. Yes, I mean, I physically cried. Friends, you're up to your elbows in alligators and crocodiles, and the last thing you want to hear from the Lord is about a great battle preparing to take place in your life.

FEAR NOT, FOR I AM with you; Be not dismayed, for I am your God. I will strengthen you, Yes, I will help you, I will uphold you with My righteous right hand.' ~ Isaiah 41:10

TICKLE MY EARS, MAYBE a little, with a feel-good word. But not a GREAT Battle!

My wife came out and saw me in tears.

"*What's the matter,*" she said.

Understand these were some incredibly difficult times. I told my wife what the Lord had told me, And she just looked at me. Then she just started to laugh. In my life at this time, I was a little lacking in the humor department. I stand there just looking at my wife, and she shakes her head.

"*Sounds like the Lord has something pretty special in mind, I don't suppose He's done with you.*" She turns to walk away and says,"*You may want to be sharpening that sword a little.*"

That is not what I was looking to hear out of her. And then if that's not enough what would become her battle cry through this entire ordeal, she turns around and says, "*Remember, I'm in the boat with you too, Jonah!*" then goes inside. I'm just left standing there, shaking my head. Lord, Lord, really all of this.

It didn't take long for life to bite me again. It happened on a late evening when a state trooper came to the door. Showing a warrant where I was charged for Construction Fraud for one of the projects I had been unable to return the money on. The projects had been started but not completed, so I was still responsible for returning all monies on an uncompleted project, even funds that had already been spent and gone into the project. However, I had previously entered into an agreement for repayment back to the homeowner before any of this went to the courts. But the downturn ended up being worse than I estimated, and there was no work to be found.

Therefore, not sure what I'd expected, but at that very moment, when the officer had shown up, I felt like my life had been turned upside down. Before getting into the patrol car, I had a moment of prayer as we got ready to leave. Okay, God, if this is it, so be it. God works in peculiar ways. Even as this officer was doing his job, I knew he was just the messenger. I believe the Lord was able to touch him, and we had a good conversation. If that's even possible when being arrested. It turns out, as I get to the jail, there are about five other officers standing in there waiting for me to come through the door. I am a big man, but not that big. Lord, we didn't need all of this, I thought. The head man is standing there and sees me come through the door.

He starts laughing and says, "*What in the world are you doing here?*"

I smiled and thought, okay, God, I needed this. I think my regular rate of breathing had come back to me by then.

I looked over at the deputy and replied, "*When I shut the construction business down, I had some unfinished business to take care of,*" then smiled.

In the meantime, I had to wait for the Magistrate to show up to address the issue of bail. The arresting officer gave me do's and don'ts for addressing the Magistrate, and in the meantime, I stood talking with the other officers while I waited. In my world, the extent of mishaps requiring the judicial system had included two traffic tickets in thirty years. So, for the most part, I was pretty much a straight shooter. Magistrate shows up, and everything was taken care of, I'm free on my own recognizance. There was nothing pleasant about any of this. My saving grace in all of this was faith and prayer. I had built a house for the head man there. And his number two man was my son's neighbor, and I knew the other officer. So God was working. That night when I walked out of the sheriff's office my wife was there in the car, waiting. My wife called a friend of ours at the church, and he informed her of what I was going through and that it would soon be over, and I would be released. I don't think I said ten words worth repeating all the way home that night. Not what I'd expected. But the battle was just beginning. Of course, by now, with no work, my house had gone into foreclosure. And in my mind, I kept saying, "*When do we get to the part about favor of the Lord?*" I had tried to keep my guys working and going where I could. But it was terrible. It seemed like everybody was losing something, houses, cars, marriages, investments. Those were unfortunate times for a whole lot of good people. I continued in prayer, and every so often, I would have another angel visitation. There were times I was questioning my sanity. Friends don't think you are going to reason with the Holy Spirit with your flesh. It's not going to work. God wasn't done. It would only be a couple of weeks before I would receive another arrest warrant for the other project. Even to this day, I stand fully accountable for what happened. Did I hate them, yep? Was I mad yep? Would I have done the same thing if I had been in their place? Probably. Bitterness can become an awful spirit of oppression if you allow it to just manifest and grow day after day. Regardless of your situation. Don't allow that bitterness to become a controlling demon in your life.

FOR WE DO NOT WRESTLE against flesh and blood, but against principalities, against powers, against the rulers of [a]the darkness of this age, against spiritual hosts of wickedness in the heavenly places. ~ Ephesians 6:12

IN TRUTH, IT WOULD become my daily battle. Don't let it become yours. Eventually, a lot of anger would leave, and I would learn humility. If I could have seen this big train wreck coming. I would have tried to do everything possible to have prevented it. Even to this day, I regret this situation and what happened to those folks. But it's part of the past, and I will not allow it to be used as a torment to shape my future.

The night of the second arrest, I thanked God for wisdom because of circumstances, I was able to go and turn myself into the authorities. I was shown the most respect through the entire situation and was able to address the matter before me. But at this point, if it wasn't for the Word of God, the relationship I had with my Heavenly Father, the extraordinary heavenly encounter I had experienced out at the cross and altar those three days and nights. I don't know what would have happened to me. It was bad. It would be a couple of months between dealing with legalities and attorneys that life kept my plate pretty full. Now do rest assured as, in the Book of Job, I was taken down to where life was no fun. There was no money and a lot of stress and my court-appointed attorney and me. Eventually, the court cases would end. I would be found guilty as accused. I offer no argument or further explanation. God knows that I did not set out to defraud these people of any money. And that's where I will rest with it.

Our home, that too , would come to settle and go to foreclosure. And in the midst of all this I would begin to find a new peace in Christ that I had never felt before. But in one of my moments of self again, I would call out to the Lord. It would be on that night when I cried out, Lord, where were you, Lord, why me? And sure enough, the Lord would send His messenger that night to give me an answer. I was really restless that night. There was so much going on. Have you ever been in that place before? It was not a happy place, and all I wanted to do was to go to bed early after a hot bath. My wife would hear me in the bathtub. Believe me, God and I had some powerful conversations on some of those nights. One in particular that was rather funny that I have to insert here is about one of those nights. The phone rings, my wife answers it's our neighbor. She wanted to know if someone was shouting outside in our field?

My wife said, "*It's just my husband getting a talking to from his Heavenly Father, that's all.*" Mrs. Baker laughed and said, "*Everybody needs a good talking to every once in a while.*" Praise God that I can still find humor in some of this.

Ok now back to when I finally went to bed that night after my bath, an angel appeared and took me on another journey. When we stopped, I was standing outside the Courthouse on the steps.

I said, "*Where has my Father been, why have I felt so alone through all of this?*" The angel stood, pointing, and said "*I was there in the courtroom, and I was standing here on these steps outside the Courthouse.*"

I was looking, while reliving the day before. And then, the angel stood and turned and faced me. "*I never left you,*" the angel said.

As he turned his arms, his stature changed. HIS arms were backed by large wings that kept expanding and expanding large enough to wrap around a car.

"*You can see in the spiritual, but yet you did not see me, and why was that?*" the angel asked.

I looked at him and thought for a second. Then I understood what he was telling me. I was allowing that of the world to cloud my vision of God. How could I expect to hear God if I could not see the evil of this world that was getting in my way? An important note here. Everyone reading this, I pray you to find your special place, your prayer closet, your prayer room, your favorite chair in the den, or out on the porch. But that place where you can go and meditate on the word of God. If you don't feed your spirit person, how do you expect to be spiritually healthy? You have to take time for you and your Heavenly Father. This is war, and the battle is for your soul.

Favor with God, Lord, what did I do to deserve so much favor? I can not exaggerate the emotions and these moments in my life. They were bad. Did I ever think I'm ready to end it and call it quits? I would be lying to you if I told you I didn't. There were nights that I had tears, asking how I got here? How I got to this point and time in my life. Life became one big reflection of looking into the mirror. But Lord, this can't be happening to me. I'm the guy that has all the angelic visitations, and we have shared so much Lord, you have shown me many great things that are and yet to come. Why Lord? Oh, how I almost tear up as I write these words thinking about what I was going through at that time. Oh, how much my flesh was wanting to reason and question everything. Everything I had been through kept playing and replaying through my head. I knew my faith was getting forged in the fires of Heavens. God knew, God always knows. Friends, don't you ever doubt it either. We have a loving Father that knows. HE will take you, and HE will bring you through. You will be molded as raw clay from the earth, and you will be tested by fire in the furnaces of life, so hot, you will think there can be no God. See again, God would use the situation and circumstances to cut to my very marrow in my bones. God will break you until you are HIS.

BUT NOW, O LORD, YOU are our Father; We are the clay, and You our potter; And all we are the work of Your hand. ~Isaiah 64:8

I HAD A DECISION TO make at this point, and as a pastor friend pointed out, saying to me, "You can be pitiful or powerful, you choose." I chose to be powerful. It would be a couple of months later, and things were pretty heated up. Days ran into days. And even putting my feet on the ground became hard. Eventually, I would end up ready to check out of this big world. It was pretty bad. It was about 11:00 a.m that I was awakened with the dog licking me on the face because he needed to go out. But I didn't feel so good. My wife was not there; she had gone to an appointment. So I had continued to lay in bed. I remembered that during the night, I had taken several antacids to battle my indigestion. Nothing seemed to work. I felt horrible to the point I couldn't move.

With one big push from the bed to get my clothes and headed to the steps, I made it downstairs. I felt terrible. I called my wife on the phone, and she was just a few minutes away. By the time she got there, I was going in and out of consciousness from the chest pains and discomfort. After about a 20 minute ride to the ER, they took me straight back. Once they had me hooked up, they informed me that I had an irregular heartbeat, and things were far from normal. I looked at my wife, and I remember throwing her a kiss as I turned away. I was feeling pretty sick. So I asked the nurse for something in case I got sick. She hands me this tiny round blue cup to throw up in if I should need it. It turned out I wouldn't need it. See, I died there on that bed that day. I was going home. I had enough of this world. Was I selfish, was I being mean? I don't know; I was dead. So here I am writing to you about my story from the grave. I bet you weren't expecting that one? Laugh out loud! Well, things sometimes don't go the way we expect them to, do they? Especially when God is involved. So there I go walking down this long hall, and I can see someone sitting at a table. There beside him was this long corridor, with a very bright light. I'm on my way. I see the man stand and come out from around the table, and he looks at me and asks, "*What are you doing here?*"

"*I am going to be with my Father,*" I replied.

Casting a long glancing look down the long corridor, I started walking toward the very bright light.

"*No!*" he shouts,

"*That is not your decision to make.*" as he moves closer to me.

Pushing against me, saying, "*You have to go back!*"

"*No!*" I replied, "*I'm not going back!*"

The man walks to me and tells me, "*The Father has much work for you yet to do!*"

Again pushing me back two more times. I nodded at his request, and as I turned, I felt a tear coming down my cheek. I turned to go back and there on the wall, or Heaven's doorway, was a large zig-zag of bright light, it was like I was about to step into a large lighting bolt passageway. As I stepped through and turned to look back, there standing was the Son of God with a lamb cradled in His arms. He pointed at me to go back. I then step back into life. I was awakened lying on the table in the ER with about 12 people or so around me, shouting in my ear. I was gasping for air. My wife, she was outside the room in

Holy Ghost prayer, and that day, the Lord would heal me and bring me back to this life. The following day the doctor would examine my heart. As I walked into the room, the nurse had already told the doctor about what had happened.

The doctor looks at me and grins saying, "*I understand you were the talk of the hospital yesterday.*" I just nodded.

Looking at the doctor, I told him that the Lord had healed me, and I felt alright. Maybe not what you say to a doctor about to check you out. He looks at me and tells me he would determine if God had healed me. So up on the treadmill, I go. I begin walking, and there's no pain. The speed of the treadmill and slope increase, but all feels good. After the test is completed, the doctor begins looking things over. Then the doctor just looks up at me.

He stood there for a moment shaking his head and said, "*For somebody that was the talk of the hospital yesterday, well, you sure are healed today. For all my years of doing this, your numbers may not be perfect, but they're close enough, I believe you were healed!*" And he turned and walked out of the room.

The nurse said, "*I told him, I told him you were healed!*" and I just smiled.

Thank you and Amen Lord! After my release from the hospital driving home, all of a sudden, I realized those things in life that mattered didn't. Life seemed different. I still had the issues in life, but it became just another day.

See self will holler and scream and not want to let go. Self dies hard; it was a learning-teaching process. But your knees will bend. I think at this point, when I went into that refiner's fire of life, no matter how terrible, how horrific the situations were, Did it hurt? But did it? Or was it just the flesh dying to self, giving way to those things of God and what HE was showing me. The same way, He will show you.

AND I WILL BRING THE third part through the fire and will refine them as silver is refined, and will try them as gold is tried: they shall call on my name, and I will hear them: I will say, It is my people: and they shall say, The Lord is my God. ~ Zechariah 13:9

Chapter 12

The Power of Prayer

In this final chapter of this book I want to take you back to when I was a young teenager. I had a beautiful German shepherd that went everywhere I went. His name was Prince. Prince lived a long life. And as he got older, he started getting in pretty bad shape. Mom had told me we were going to have to put the old dog down. Feeling heavy-hearted, I told mom I would put him down and bury him in the woods where we had hunted all of those years. So down through the woods, I go. Shovel in one hand, gun in the other, and my dog following me. Now the more I dug that hole, the heavier that shovel full of dirt would get. When ole Prince came over and laid on the pile of dirt that was coming out of his grave I started to tear up. And eventually, I realized I wasn't going to be able to do this. So back up to the house, I went. When I walked into the house, Mom just looked at me.

She smiled and then shook her head and said, *"I didn't think you could do that when you loved something as long as you have that dog, it makes it hard to let go."*

I looked at Mom and said, *"I don't know what to do?"*

Mom looked at me and replied, *"Maybe you should ask God!"*

See, Mom had a heart problem I didn't know about. Eventually, we took the dog to the vet to have him put to sleep. And Dad had to do it.

Now fast forward several years to one night in October of 1980. We are at Jones's funeral home in our hometown, and Mom was hugging onto a casket crying. That was when my brother was killed, and at that moment, our lives had gotten a little bit harder. In fact, that would have a significant effect on our family for as long as mom and dad lived. Folks hadn't arrived at the funeral home yet, and Mom was crying.

No, she was sobbing, saying, *"I don't know what I'm going to do?"*

And at that moment, I would remember what Mom had told me about that ole dog.

I looked at Mom and said, *"Why don't you ask God what you should do?"* Mom stopped crying, came over, and hugged me. See friends Mom had a heart condition. I had no relationship with God. Where was God in my life? I would come to ask myself days later. But I never forgot what Mom had told me years before about that pet of mine that I had loved so much. Over the years, the devil would come to kill, steal, and destroy our family.

A couple of days before my dad would die from pancreatic cancer. Dad called me in to sit down and talk with him. He said I need you to do something for me. See friends by this time our family had really started to come under awful attacks.

Dad looked at me and said, *"I want you to do whatever you have to do to make sure your mother doesn't have to bury another child."*

Eventually, I would tell mom what dad had asked of me. Only after I had done what he had asked. Like trying to prevent my younger sister from dying from a heroin overdose. And those were challenging times. My mom, she never gave up. No matter what happened in life or how hard that devil tried to destroy our family. Mom never let it get to her. Our mom really did have a heart problem. See friends, Mom had a love of Christ on the inside of her heart. And it gave her the strength to deal with the attacks of the devil against our family. I share this with you all , because when it came time for Mom to go home to be with the Lord. I, too, realized I had a heart problem.

Friends, I don't want to see anybody here have to lie across a casket crying or deal with the issues that are destroying families without having a heart problem. The Book of Romans tells us, 'If God is for us who can be against us.' His name is Jesus, do you know Him? I want everybody to believe in God's authority over their family.

"SUBMIT YOURSELVES THEREFORE to God. Resist the devil, and he will flee from you." ~ James 4:7

FRIENDS, THIS WORLD is moving at such a fast pace. World events that take place across the planet can be seen only minutes after they have happened. If one country in the world sneezes, the entire world is catching a cold. With unstable governments and extreme radicalism of populations, the evil of hate grows. These are the end times our Bible has told us about. The good of Christ is becoming more and more hidden, as this evil is running wild across the world. How often did we hear wars and rumors of wars? Friends, we are there, this One World clock is ticking! You know the alternative, without Christ, there can be no peace. How many times will we watch terrorist bombs exploding, destroying the innocence of life? All in the name of an extreme belief, or a call for injustice committed against an entire population. Shock waves of hate that result in all people feeling the pain of cowardly acts of suicide. With only one goal, to destroy this life and world we once knew. Where suffering and death are shared over the information highway. Oh, how many will say, "Where was God?" Or perhaps say, "Why would God even allow this?" Friends, God will never take away the free will of mankind. These are the times where we need to pay attention! And not be looking to the problem solvers of the world to end this hellish behavior that attacks this world like a plague. But seek God and keep our eyes on Him. Without your spiritual glasses on you will only be blinded by what the world wants you to see. Didn't God warn us? I often ponder this, but the question will become. As children of God did we heed His warning. Did we recognize the nuggets that God has always given us?

How much blood will be shed and how many victims? Have we already become victims of this evil taking over this world? Will the echo of children dying in the carnage and seeing so much evil around us be enough to trigger the one last great revival before the return of Christ? The world wants you to learn how to live and cope with the pain of this world. But these are all pains that are only temporary. We know God will bring the evil of this world to an end. No matter how depressing this world becomes, this evil world has already been defeated by Jesus Christ. Will we question our faith? Will your confidence have grown in God's strength as you have learned to hear the Holy Spirit whispering in your ear? I pray my words have caused you to examine and grow your faith only stronger and stronger. Because you are going to need it. With the impossible situations to come, that this world has never experienced. The One World Government and Antichrist have to prevail. Birthed from the evil that has been prophesied from generations until the return of Christ. You will need unshakeable faith.

For if you don't accept the responsibility to build your faith in Christ for you and your family, the outcome for you and your family will be one of chaos and fear. This world never offered us the safety and security we thought it did. It can only come from that relationship of real intimacy with your Heavenly Father. Throughout this book, I have emphasized the problems that we will all soon face. It didn't matter whether I offended you, or these words provoked fear. These words were divinely given to challenge you. To support you in the strengthening of your faith. The world in the short time that you have read this book will have changed. World wide shocking events will have become more and more of the norm on your TV. For most people, they will go into this world without a strategy for themselves or their families. Only a faith forged in the fires from God with grace will prevail. No matter how big any man's army is. Or how life-saving a new medicine may be. It will never be enough. It is only the safety and security you will find in your faith in God. A faith that can only come from you accepting Christ Jesus as Lord and Savior of your life. Come quickly Lord, I pray.

See, friend's time is running out. When life causes you or a loved one to suffer, or you're hanging over the casket of a child. I only pray that you will have a heart condition. Yes, A Heart Condition! Where your faith in Jesus Christ will give you the greatest blessing from your salvation. Regardless of the challenges, and hardships, this world brings upon your family.

Maybe God was absent in your family? Perhaps you didn't know that your Great-Grandmother read and studied the word of God. Perhaps you weren't aware of how much a family member had studied God's word and was blessed by the word of God? In those hardships of life, your mom and dad dealt with, did they cry out to God? Maybe you don't know, but I can tell you this. If you're reading this and you've never had that walk or relationship of intimacy with Jesus Christ. Somebody prayed for you. Someone's prayers were answered. Do you really think this is by chance? See, in Heaven, we know those who cry out to God, do not go unanswered. Oh, how many I have seen that question how they found their walk with Christ when no one in the family ever had. You think because you have walked in some ungodly hellish situation, you came to Christ? No. That was just the fuse that had to be lit in this world to bring you to your knees. To break that flesh, to allow the Holy Spirit to work in you. Friends, please never underestimate the power of prayer. Prayer that has been planted on your behalf over the generations, whether from family or friends. Where they too shared tears from pain from the challenges of life in their walks on this earth. How important it is for you to pray this forward for family and friends. That is what has happened to me; someone prayed for me. Actually, the breakthrough that put an end to the torment of the 2008 downturn of my life came from prayer. Let me explain. One afternoon while in prayer, crying out for a breakthrough, it just seemed like my prayers were being held up. I then recalled a bible study from the book of Daniel, chapter 10. Where there was a great battle going on in the Heavenly over Daniel's prayer being held up for 21 days by evil. It took the Archangels Michael and Gabriel to get the breakthrough. So, I prayed harder. Then it happened...breakthrough. God sent a fine gentleman into our life who had bought my wife's beautiful art on the internet. He just happened to be in the area on business, (he's a Vice President of Marketing Affiliations for a major Christian Cable Company) so he called and wanted to meet his artist. After a very delightful lunch and an afternoon of sharing, he said on his next trip to Jerusalem, he would put our names in the Western Wall for prayer.

"It's a local call to God there 24/7!" He said with a smile.

Well, Glory Be To God, Hallelujah, it worked! After that, things started turning around and are getting better. I thank God for this man and his obedience to come to visit, not knowing anything about our situation. THAT'S HOW GOD WORKS! Yep, an on-time God! He, too, will answer your prayers! Just trust Him. The Power of Prayer, never underestimate it.

I can never overemphasize. This is how the Kingdom of God works. It's amazing, incredible, supernatural. Stop trying to figure it out. Don't get religious, just know that God has given you that wonderful gift of Salvation and the Power of Prayer. Kingdom authority to pray it forward for your family. You've read what is coming. So pray and plant that seed for future generations? That they, too, will see the Kingdom of God. When hell is breaking loose upon the face of this earth. You can believe somewhere, sometime, someone prayed for you. It doesn't matter who or even if you know. What matters is you are here reading this now. Friends, the clock is ticking; it's not too late. Repeat after me...

FOR GOD SO LOVED THE world that He gave His only begotten Son, that whoever believes in Him should not perish but have everlasting life.~ John 3:16

WALK IN THE KINGDOM of Jesus Christ with me.

Don't miss out!

Visit the website below and you can sign up to receive emails whenever R.J. Manuel publishes a new book. There's no charge and no obligation.

https://books2read.com/r/B-A-PNBK-XLEEB

BOOKS 2 READ

Connecting independent readers to independent writers.

About the Author

Robert J. Manuel became a Minister after a life of unpredictable twists and turns. A Bible teacher, a sharer of the word of God, assisting and working with the homeless, lifting up those in need. After attending Bethlehem Bible College later in life, he realized a day was coming that he would share with the world about his Angelic Visitations and Global Events to come. He has been Blessed with Gifts of the Spirit that allowed him to see where the demonic dwell. His theology is not about the religious but a practical, down to earth approach to helping the need of all people. He believes that Deliverance comes from God's love, and people will be set free.

Read more at https://angelicvisitations.com/.